Also by David DeFord

Ordinary People Can Achieve the Extraordinary –
A Practical Guide to Goal Achievement

1000 Brilliant Achievement Quotes

Advice from the World's Wisest

by David DeFord

Ordinary People Can Win!
Omaha, NE

To Fred DeFord, my dad, who taught me about loyalty, integrity and true success.

Ordinary People Can Win is dedicated to helping ordinary people achieve extraordinary successes in all areas of their lives.

We encourage personal development, living with integrity, and giving back to the community.

Our main areas of focus are:

Website

Found at www.OrdinaryPeopleCanWin.com our website provides 200 pages of information that will help you get what you want. It offers:

a)   Dozens of articles on personal development, integrity, volunteering, and more

b)   Inspirational stories of everyday heroes

c)   Resources from success mentors

d)   Inspirational quotes

e)   Links to other excellent achievement web resources

You will find our site refreshing, encouraging and filled with helpful information.

Free, weekly e-zine

Our e-zine will help you break free from your limiting beliefs, remind you of what you want, and give you insight into ways to move forward.

Some past issues have featured articles that teach:

- Why settle for what you have?
- Eleven steps to get what you want
- Changing wishes into decisions
- To change yourself, change your environment

Subscribe to this free e-zine at: **www.ordinarypeoplecanwin.com**

Free achievement e-course

This 6-lesson course, *Ordinary People Can Achieve*, will help you change your approaches and achieve true successes.

Spend a half-hour every other day, and you'll find yourself well on your way to achieving your goals.

Lesson 1: Introduction

Lesson 2: Selecting Goals

Lesson 3: Why Do You Want to Achieve It?

Lesson 4: Visualize Your Success

Lesson 5: Reviewing Progress

Lesson 6: Conclusion

To register for this free course, send a blank email to: ordinarypeople@getresponse.com

Speaking engagements

Ordinary People Can Win owner, David DeFord, will speak to your organization at no charge.

He can address any of the following topics:

- Living with significance
- True success depends upon integrity
- You can make a difference in this world
- Ordinary People Can Achieve the Extraordinary

David stresses volunteerism and vigorously encourages the audience to support and work at your organization's service efforts.

He communicates the need to find more meaning and purpose in life through means other than careers and the "TV existence."

To discuss a possible speaking opportunity, contact David at ddeford@ordinarypeoplecanwin.com

Book publishing

The next book by David DeFord will be *Ordinary People Can Live with Extraordinary Significance*. Keep watching our website or e-zine for the release date.

We are looking for authors who would like to write how-to books for the *Ordinary People Can....*series. Future books in this series include:

+ Ordinary People Can Publish an Extraordinary Book
+ Ordinary People Can Publish an Extraordinary E-zine
+ Ordinary People Can Run a Marathon
+ Ordinary People Can.....

If you have an expertise and would like to be published in ebook and/or print form, contact us at info@OrdinaryPeopleCanWin.com.

About the Author

David DeFord has studied personal development all of his adult life. Having discovered Dale Carnegie, Napoleon Hill, and Dr. Norman Vincent Peale as a young man, he has read and put into practice many of the teachings of the greatest motivational teachers of our time.

A frequent and popular speaker, he has honed his talents over the years. His enthusiasm and passion lifts his audiences.

A long-time information technology executive, David has served as manager, director, vice president, and officer of regional corporations.

In 2003, David turned a disappointing job loss into a successful entrepreneur venture with Ordinary People Can Win. He publishes the website http://www.OrdinaryPeopleCanWin.com and its companion electronic newsletter. He also speaks to civic and service organizations as well as corporations and conventions regarding achievement, living with passion and compassion, giving back to the community, and living with integrity.

David has been married to the love of his life, Kathy, since 1972. They have four children, and several grandchildren. They actively participate in church and volunteer organizations.

DeFord also authored *Ordinary People Can Achieve the Extraordinary—A Practical Guide to Goal Achievement*. You can find it on Amazon.com

To receive weekly inspiration and insights into how you can live your dreams and live with significance, subscribe to our free e-zine Ordinary People Can Win. To subscribe, go to http://www.OrdinaryPeopleCanWin.com/ezinepage.htm

Table of Contents

Introduction

Each of us needs encouragement. As we face obstacles to our integrity and our personal progress we often look to the advice of the wisest. This volume provides the most brilliant wisdom regarding achievement handed down over the ages.

From slugger Henry Aaron to Carl Zuckermeyer, Anne Frank to George Burns, wise people have offered wonderful and useful advice on successful living.

I have sifted through tens of thousands of quotes, reluctantly discarding most of them, in an effort to bring you the most brilliant of them.

You may wish to use this volume as a reference work. But I encourage you to read it from cover to cover initially. Like eating hot cayenne pepper sauce, the effect of reading powerful quotes produces an accumulated potency. The more you read, the stronger the impact.

To further your study of these great individuals you can go to a special web page developed to give you more information about the individual. Simply go to http://www.ordinarypeoplecanwin/1000achievement.htm.

On this page you will find links to books and other resources by the person. I encourage you to dig deeply and achieve your dreams!

Achievement

"Never mistake activity for achievement."

John Wooden

"A non-doer is very often a critic-that is, someone who sits back and watches doers, and then waxes philosophically about how the doers are doing. It's easy to be a critic, but being a doer requires effort, risk, and change."

Dr. Wayne W. Dyer

"Hoping and dreaming of a better world are not enough if we are unwilling to work; but when we work towards our dreams, wonderful things can happen."

Lloyd Newell

"The sweetness of victory is magnified by the effort it took to achieve it."

Chris Widener

"The greater the difficulty the more glory in surmounting it. Skillful pilots gain their reputation from storms and tempests."

Epictetus

"All successful employers are stalking people who will do the unusual, people who think, people who attract attention by performing more than is expected of them."

Charles M. Schwab

"Success is not measured by what you accomplish but by the opposition you have encountered, and the courage with which you have maintained the struggle against overwhelming odds."

Orison Swett Marden

"Empty pockets never held anyone back. Only empty heads and empty hearts can do that."

Norman Vincent Peale

"We will either find a way, or make one."

Hannibal

"The only way around is through."

Robert Frost

"Great things are not done by impulse, but by a series of small things brought together."

Vincent Van Gogh

"You don't have to be a fantastic hero to do certain things— to compete. You can be just an ordinary chap, sufficiently motivated to reach challenging goals."

Sir Edmund Hillary

"My mother drew a distinction between achievement and success. She said that achievement is the knowledge that you have studied and worked hard and done the best that is in you. Success is being praised by others. That is nice but not as important or satisfying. Always aim for achievement and forget about success."

Helen Hayes

"The best job goes to the person who can get it done without passing the buck or coming back with excuses."

Napoleon Hill

"A man may fulfill the object of his existence by asking a question he cannot answer, and attempting a task he cannot achieve."

Oliver Wendell Holmes

"High achievement always takes place in a framework of high expectation."

Jack Kinder

"Man is always more than he can know of himself; consequently, his accomplishments, time and again, will come as a surprise to him."

Golo Mann

"Trust yourself. Create the kind of self that you will be happy to live with all your life. Make the most of yourself by fanning the tiny, inner sparks of possibility into flames of achievement."

Foster C. McClellan

"I am always doing things I can't do, that's how I get to do them."

Pablo Picasso

"The truth of the matter is that there's nothing you can't accomplish if:
(1) You clearly decide what it is that you're absolutely committed to achieving,
(2) You're willing to take massive action,
(3) You notice what's working or not, and
(4) You continue to change your approach until you achieve what you want, using whatever life gives you along the way."

Anthony Robbins

"The will to win, the desire to succeed, the urge to reach your full potential… these are the keys that will unlock the door to personal excellence."

Eddie Robinson

"Disciplining yourself to do what you know is right and important, although difficult, is the high road to pride, self esteem, and personal satisfaction."

Brian Tracy

"The only worthwhile achievements of man are those which are socially useful."

Alfred Adler

"Nothing splendid has ever been achieved except by those who dared believe that something inside them was superior to circumstances."

Bruce Barton

"Destiny is not a matter of chance, it is a matter of choice; it is not a thing to be waited for, it is a thing to be achieved."

William Jennings Bryan

"This became a credo of mine . . . attempt the impossible in order to improve your work."

Bette Davis

"Unless a man undertakes more than he possibly can do, he will never do all that he can."

Henry Drummond

"We succeed only as we identify in life, or in war, or in anything else, a single overriding objective, and make all other considerations bend to that one objective."

Dwight Eisenhower

"What is the recipe for successful achievement? To my mind there are just four essential ingredients: Choose a career you love . . . Give it the best there is in you . . . Seize your opportunities And be a member of the team. In no country but America, I believe, is it possible to fulfill all four of these requirements."

Benjamin Fairless

"To understand the heart and mind of a person, look not at what he has already achieved, but at what he aspires to."

Kahlil Gibran

"If we are striving, if we are working, if we are trying, to the best of our ability, to improve day by day, then we are in the line of our duty."

Heber J. Grant

"Never measure the height of a mountain, until you have reached the top. Then you will see how low it was."

Dag Hammarskjöld

"Decide what you want, decide what you are willing to exchange for it. Establish your priorities and go to work."

H. L. Hunt

"Only those who dare to fail greatly can ever achieve greatly."

Robert F. Kennedy

"Hell begins on the day when God grants us a clear vision of all that we might have achieved, of all the gifts which we might have wasted, of all that we might have done which we did not do."

Gian-Carlo Menotti

"Only if you reach the boundary will the boundary recede before you. And if you don't, if you confine your efforts, the boundary will shrink to accommodate itself to your efforts. And you can only expand your capacities by working to the very limit."

Hugh Nibley

"Achievement is largely the product of steadily raising one's levels of aspiration and expectation."

Jack Niklaus

"Achievement seems to be connected with action. Successful men and women keep moving. They make mistakes, but they don't quit."

Conrad Hilton

"Personal development is your springboard to personal excellence. Ongoing, continuous, non-stop personal development literally assures you that there is no limit to what you can accomplish."

Brian Tracy

"Unless you walk out into the unknown, the odds of making a profound difference in your life are pretty low."

Tom Peters

"For a man to achieve all that is demanded of him he must regard himself as greater than he is."

Johann Goethe

"I found that the men and women who got to the top were those who did the jobs they had in hand, with everything they had of energy and enthusiasm and hard work."

Harry S. Truman

Attitude

"Your mental attitude is something you can control outright and you must use self discipline until you create a positive mental attitude - your mental attitude attracts to you everything that makes you what you are."

Napoleon Hill

"Something happens inside of us when we are courteous and deferential toward others. It is all part of a refining process, which if persisted in, will change our very natures."

Gordon B. Hinckley

"Age is more a matter of how you feel, how you think, and what's going on in your head than what's going on in your feet—although I wouldn't want to be challenged to a foot race this morning."

Gordon B. Hinckley

"We are creatures of our thinking. We can talk ourselves into defeat or we can talk ourselves into victory."

Gordon B. Hinckley

"People rarely succeed unless they have fun in what they are doing."

Dale Carnegie

"By bravely enduring our trials, we learn humility, compassion for others, and a great reliance on God. We also learn that our happiness and progress depend much less upon what challenges life may bring and infinitely more on how we face and overcome those challenges."

Lloyd Newell

"Individuals who deliberately decide not to take offense lead happier, more productive lives."

Lloyd Newell

"Any fact facing us is not as important as our attitude toward it, for that determines our success or failure. The way you think about a fact may defeat you before you ever do anything about it. You are overcome by the fact because you think you are."

Norman Vincent Peale

"The state of your life is nothing more than a reflection of your state of mind."

Dr. Wayne W. Dyer

"If you believe you can, you probably can. If you believe you won't, you most assuredly won't. Belief is the ignition switch that gets you off the launching pad."

Denis Waitley

"Ability is what you're capable of doing. Motivation determines what you do. Attitude determines how well you do it."

Lou Holtz

"Holding on to anger is like grasping a hot coal with the intent of throwing it at someone else; you are the one who gets burned.

Buddha

"The optimist sees opportunity in every danger; the pessimist sees danger in every opportunity."

Winston Churchill

"Our attitudes control our lives. Attitudes are a secret power working twenty-four hours a day, for good or bad. It is of paramount importance that we know how to harness and control this great force."

Tom Blandi

"A great attitude does much more than turn on the lights in our worlds; it seems to magically connect us to all sorts of serendipitous opportunities that were somehow absent before the change."

Earl Nightingale

"Positive thinking won't let you do anything but it will let you do everything better than negative thinking will."

Zig Ziglar

"It's not what happens to you that determines how far you will go in life; it is how you handle what happens to you."

Zig Ziglar

"The door to a balanced success opens widest on the hinges of hope and encouragement."

Zig Ziglar

"The greatest discovery of my generation is that human beings can alter their lives by altering their attitudes of mind."

William James

"Wondrous is the strength of cheerfulness, and its power of endurance—the cheerful man will do more in the same time, will do it better, will preserve it longer, than the sad or sullen."

Thomas Carlyle

"Cheerfulness is the off-shoot of goodness."

Christian Nestell Bovee

"Eagles come in all shapes and sizes, but you will recognize them chiefly by their attitudes."
Charles Prestwich Scott

"I am convinced that attitude is the key to success or failure in almost any of life's endeavors. Your attitude-your perspective, your outlook, how you feel about yourself, how you feel about other people-determines your priorities, your actions, your values. Your attitude determines how you interact with other people and how you interact with yourself."
Carolyn Warner

"Attitude is more important than the past, than education, than money, than circumstances, than what people do or say. It is more important than appearance, giftedness, or skill."
Charles Swindoll

"I believe life is to be lived, not worked, enjoyed, not agonized, loved, not hated."
Leland Bartlett

"Happiness is not by chance, but by choice."
Jim Rohn

"Most of us are only six inches away from success; the distance between our ears."
Dave Cole

"Spare yourselves from the indulgence of self-pity. It is always self-defeating. Subdue the negative and emphasize the positive."

Gordon B. Hinckley

"Do, or do not. There is no try"

Yoda

"A positive attitude may not solve all your problems, but it will annoy enough people to make it worth the effort."

Herm Albright

"Positive thinking will let you do everything better than negative thinking will."

Dean Naylor

"It's not the situation. . . . It's your reaction to the situation."

Robert Conklin

"If things are not going well with you, begin your effort at correcting the situation by carefully examining the service you are rendering, and especially the spirit in which you are rendering it."

Roger Ward Babson

"A happy person is not a person in a certain set of circumstances, but rather a person with a certain set of attitudes."

Hugh Downs

"Attitude is an important part of the foundation upon which we build a productive life. A good attitude produces good results, a fair attitude poor results, a poor attitude poor results. We each shape our own life, and the shape of it is determined largely by our attitude.

M. Russell Ballard

"If you could change anything about the way you approach selling, the thing that will make the biggest difference would be your attitude - your attitude toward your customers, your service, the benefits of your products, your employer, and yourself."

Dan Brent Burt

"There are two big forces at work, external and internal. We have very little control over external forces such as tornadoes, earthquakes, floods, disasters, illness and pain. What really matters is the internal force. How do I respond to those disasters? Over that I have complete control."

Leo F. Buscalgia

"You can't build a great company without great people. But how do you know them when you see them? Over the past few years, a number of companies in a wide range of industries - from airlines to steel, computers to hotels – have asked themselves what separates their winners from their losers, good hires from bad, and they all arrived at the same answer: what people know is less important than who they are. Hiring, they believe, is not about finding people with the right experience; it's about finding people with the right mind-set. These companies hire for attitude and train for skill."

Peter Carbonara

"You are as young as your faith, as old as your doubt, as young as your self-confidence, as old as your fear, as young as your hope, as old as your despair."

Paul H. Dunn

"Weakness of attitude becomes weakness of character."

Albert Einstein

"I never saw a pessimistic general win a battle."

Dwight Eisenhower

"The long span of the bridge of your life is supported by countless cables called habits, attitudes, and desires. What you do in life depends upon what you are and what you want. What you get from life depends upon how much you want it-how much you are willing to work and plan and cooperate and use your resources. The long span of the bridge of your life is supported by countless cables that you are spinning now, and that is why today is such an important day. Make the cables strong!"

L.G. Elliott

"Most men in a concentration camp believed that the real opportunities of life had passed. Yet, in reality, there was an opportunity and a challenge. One could make a victory of those experiences, turning life into an inner triumph, or one could ignore the challenge and simply vegetate, as did a majority of the prisoners."

Viktor Frankl

"The last of the human freedoms is to choose one's attitude in any given set of circumstances."

Viktor Frankl

"The only disability in life is a bad attitude."

Scott Hamilton

"We who lived in concentration camps can remember those who walked through the huts comforting others, giving away their last piece of bread. They may have been few in number, but they offer sufficient proof that everything can be taken from a person but the last of the human freedoms - to choose one's attitude in any given set of circumstances - to choose one's own way."

Viktor Frankl

"Each experience through which we pass operates ultimately for our good. This is a correct attitude to adopt and we must be able to see it in that light."

Raymond Holliwell

"Character is the result of two things: mental attitude and the way we spend our time."

Elbert Hubbard

"Human beings can alter their lives by altering their attitudes of mind."

William James

"It is our attitude at the beginning of a difficult task which, more than anything else, will affect its successful outcome."

William James

"Nothing can stop the man with the right mental attitude from achieving his goal; nothing on earth can help the man with the wrong mental attitude."

Thomas Jefferson

"Keep your face to the sunshine and you cannot see the shadow."

Helen Keller

"People are just about as happy as they make up their minds to be."

Abraham Lincoln

"Things turn out best for the people who make the best of the way things turn out."

Art Linkletter

"At the center of our agency is our freedom to form a healthy attitude toward whatever circumstances we are placed in!"

Neal A. Maxwell

"With confidence, you can reach truly amazing heights; without confidence, even the simplest accomplishments are beyond your grasp."

Jim Loehr

"Your living is determined not so much by what life brings to you as by the attitude you bring to life; not so much by what happens to you as by the way your mind looks at what happens."

John Homer Miller

"If you will call your troubles experiences, and remember that every experience develops some latent force within you, you will grow vigorous and happy, however adverse your circumstances may seem to be."

James Russell Miller

"Our attitude toward life determines life's attitude towards us."

Earl Nightingale

"Success or failure in business is caused more by the mental attitude even than by mental capacities."

Sir Walter Scott

"Adopting the right attitude can convert a negative stress into a positive one."

Hans Selye

"It is a sheer waste of time and soul-power to imagine what I would do if things were different. They are not different."

Frank Crane

"THE MAN WHO THINKS HE CAN:
If you think you are beaten, you are,
If you think that you dare not, you don't,
If you'd like to win, but you think you can't,
It's almost certain you won't.
If you think you'll lose, you've lost,
For out in the world you'll find,
Success begins with a fellow's will,
It's all in the state of mind.
If you think you are outclassed, you are,
You've got to think high to rise,
You've got to be sure of yourself before
You can ever win a prize.
Life's battles don't always go
To the stronger or faster man,
But soon or late the man who wins
Is the man who thinks he can."

Arnold Palmer

"The longer I live the more I realize the impact of
attitude on life. Attitude, to me, is more important than
facts. It is more important than the past, than education,
than money, than circumstances, than failures, than
successes, than what other people think or say or do. It is
more important than appearance, giftedness or skill. It
will make or break a company . . . a church . . . a home."

Charles Swindoll

"There is little difference in people but that little difference makes a big difference. The little difference is attitude. The big difference is whether it is positive or negative."

W. Clement Stone

"The remarkable thing we have is a choice every day regarding the attitude we will embrace for that day. We cannot change our past... We cannot change the fact that people will act in a certain way. We cannot change the inevitable. The only thing we can do is play on the one string we have, and that is our attitude."

Charles Swindoll

"Words can never adequately convey the incredible impact of our attitude toward life. The longer I live the more convinced I become that life is 10 percent what happens to us and 90 percent how we respond to it."

Charles Swindoll

"The world is a looking glass and gives back to every man the reflection of his own face."

William Makepeace Thackeray

"I've never been poor, only broke. Being poor is a frame of mind. Being broke is only a temporary situation."

Mike Todd

"Develop an attitude of gratitude, and give thanks for everything that happens to you, knowing that every step forward is a step toward achieving something bigger and better than your current situation."

Brian Tracy

"Whatever is expressed is impressed. Whatever you say to yourself, with emotion, generates thoughts, ideas and behaviors consistent with those words."

Brian Tracy

"Be not afraid of life. Believe that life is worth living and your belief will help create the fact."

William James

"The real voyage of discovery consists not in making new landscapes but in having new eyes."

Marcel Proust

"Nurture your mind with great thoughts, for you will never go any higher than you think."

Benjamin Disraeli

"You can do anything if you have enthusiasm. Enthusiasm is the yeast that makes your hopes rise to the stars. With it, there is accomplishment. Without it there are only alibis."

Henry Ford

"Your own mind is a sacred enclosure into which nothing harmful can enter except by your permission."
Ralph Waldo Emerson

"When you believe you can-you can!"
Maxwell Maltz

"They are able because they think they are able."
Virgil

"The actions of men are the best interpreters of their thoughts."
John Locke

"Every memorable act in the history of the world is a triumph of enthusiasm. Nothing great was ever achieved without it because it gives any challenge or any occupation, no matter how frightening or difficult, a new meaning. Without enthusiasm you are doomed to a life of mediocrity but with it you can accomplish miracles."
Og Mandino

"You can not make excuses and money at the same time."
Dean Naylor

Character

"Character is the result of hundreds and hundreds of choices you make that gradually turn who you are, at any given moment, into who you want to be."

Jim Rohn

"Always do right - this will gratify some and astonish the rest."

Mark Twain

"Your reputation is in the hands of others. That's what a reputation is. You can't control that. The only thing you can control is your character."

Dr. Wayne W. Dyer

"Circumstances do not make a man, they reveal him."

Dr. Wayne W. Dyer

"Without preservation and cultivation of the spiritual, your material success will be as ashes in your mouths."

Gordon B. Hinckley

"How great a thing is charity, whether it be expressed through the giving of one's substance, the lending of one's strength to lift the burdens of others, or as an expression of kindness and appreciation."

Gordon B. Hinckley

"Beyond your regular vocational duties are responsibilities toward others—toward the community, the state, the nation, society in general, and the Church of which most of you are members. The attention you give to these, the energy you devote to these are of the essence of your character and your virtue."

Gordon B. Hinckley

"Trust and accountability are two great words by which we must guide our lives if we are to live beyond ourselves and rise to higher planes of service."

Gordon B. Hinckley

"The greatest work in all the world is the building of men and women of character. Without character there is not much that is worthwhile."

Ezra Taft Benson

"There are really only three kinds of people. Those who don't succeed, those who achieve success temporarily, and those who become and remain successful. Having character is the only way to sustain success. No matter how talented or rich or attractive people are, they will not be able to outrun their character.

John C. Maxwell

"Always be loyal to those who are absent, if you want to retain those who are present."

Stephen Covey

"People of poor character tend to blame their choices on circumstances. Ethical people make good choices regardless of circumstances. If they make enough good choices, they begin to create better conditions for themselves."

John C. Maxwell

"To be accounted trustworthy, a person must be predictable. When you manage your life and all the little decisions by one guideline--the Golden Rule--you create an ethical predictability in your life. People will have confidence in you, knowing that you consistently do the right thing.

John C. Maxwell

"If standard of living is your major objective, quality of life almost never improves, but if quality of life is your number one objective, your standard of living almost always improves."

Zig Ziglar

"Ability can take you to the top, but it takes character to keep you there."

Zig Ziglar

"What you do off the job is the determining factor in how far you go on the job."

Zig Ziglar

"If you don't like who you are and where you are, don't worry about it because you're not stuck either with who you are or where you are. You can grow. You can change. You can be more than you are."

Zig Ziglar

"Principle--particularly moral principle--can never be a weather vane, spinning around this way and that with the shifting winds of expediency. Moral principle is a compass forever fixed and forever true--and that is as important in business as it is in the classroom."

Edward R. Lyman

"To give real service you must add something which cannot be bought or measured with money, and that is sincerity and integrity."

Donald A. Adams

"People often say that this or that person has not yet found himself. But the self is not something one finds, it is something one creates."

Thomas Szasz

"Of all the properties which belong to honorable men, not one is so highly prized as that of character."

Henry Clay

"It is better to be faithful than famous."

Theodore Roosevelt

"It's really a wonder that I haven't dropped all my ideals, because they seem so absurd and impossible to carry out. Yet I keep them, because in spite of everything I still believe that people are really good at heart."

Anne Frank

"Character cannot be developed in ease and quiet. Only through experiences of trial and suffering can the soul be strengthened, vision cleared, ambition inspired and success achieved."

Helen Keller

"Who you are speaks so loudly I can't hear what you're saying."

Ralph Waldo Emerson

"Be kind, for everyone you meet is fighting a harder battle."

Plato

"Do right. Do your best. Treat others as you want to be treated."

Lou Holtz

"Regardless of circumstances, each man lives in a world of his own making."

Josepha Murray Emms

"Curiosity is one of the permanent and certain characteristics of a vigorous intellect."

Samuel Johnson

"A man never stands as tall as when he kneels to help a child."

The Knights of Pythagoras

"Glass, china, and reputation are easily cracked and never well mended."

Old Folk Saying

"Men of genius are admired, men of wealth are envied, men of power are feared; but only men of character are trusted."

Alfred Adler

"Don't accept that others know you better than yourself. Work joyfully and peacefully, knowing that right thoughts and right efforts will inevitably bring about right results."

James Allen

"If you are not leaning, no one will let you down."

Dr. Robert Anthony

"Whether you be man or woman you will never do anything in this world without courage. It is the greatest quality of the mind next to honor."

James Allen

"The moment a question comes to your mind, see yourself mentally taking hold of it and disposing of it. In that moment is your choice made. Thus you learn to take the path to the right. Thus you learn to become the decider and not the vacillator. Thus you build character."

H. Van Anderson

"Dignity does not consist in possessing honors, but in deserving them."

Aristotle

"Such as are thy habitual thoughts, such also will be the character of thy soul-for the soul is dyed by the thoughts. Dye it then, with a continuous series of such thoughts as these-that where a man can live, there if he will, he can also live well."

Marcus Antonius

"No man can tell whether he is rich or poor by turning to his ledger. It is the heart that makes a man rich. He is rich according to what he is, not according to what he has."

Henry Ward Beecher

"Thought creates character."

Annie Bessant

"Character may be manifested in the great moments, but it is made in the small ones."

Phillips Brooks

"Even as water carves monuments of stone, so do our thoughts shape our character.

Hugh B. Brown

"Some day, in years to come, you will be wrestling with the great temptation, or trembling under the great sorrow of your life. But the real struggle is here, now, in these quiet weeks. Now it is being decided whether, in the day of your supreme sorrow or temptation, you shall miserably fail or gloriously conquer. Character cannot be made except by a steady, long-continued process."

Phillips Brooks

"The higher up you go, the more gentle you have to reach down to help other people succeed."

Rick Castro

"After I'm dead I'd rather have people ask why I have no monument than why I have one."

Cato the Elder

"Of all the properties which belong to honorable men, not one is so highly prized as that of character."

Henry Clay

"Our own heart, and not other men's opinions, forms our true honor."

Samuel Taylor Coleridge

"Responsibility is the thing people dread most of all. Yet it is the one thing in the world that develops us, gives us manhood or womanhood fiber."

Dr. Frank Crane

"Character isn't inherited. One builds it daily by the way one thinks and acts, thought by thought, action by action. If one lets fear or hate or anger take possession of the mind, they become self-forged chains."

Helen Douglas

"Character—the willingness to accept responsibility for one's own life—is the source from which self-respect springs."

Joan Didion

"The surest way to know our gold, is to look upon it and examine it in God's furnace, where he tries it that we may see what it is. If we have a mind to know whether a building stands strong or not, we must look upon it when the wind blows. If we would know whether a staff be strong, or a rotten, broken reed, we must observe it when it is leaned on and weight is borne upon it. If we would weigh ourselves justly we must weigh ourselves in God's scales that he makes use of to weigh us."

Jonathan Edwards

"Good character is more to be praised than outstanding talent. Most talents are, to some extent, a gift. Good character, by contrast, is not given to us. We have build it piece by piece—by thought, choice, courage and determination."

John Luther

"Weakness of attitude becomes weakness of character."

Albert Einstein

"If you would not be known to do anything, never do it."

Ralph Waldo Emerson

"Make the most of yourself, for that is all there is of you."

Ralph Waldo Emerson

"Self-trust is the essence of heroism."

Ralph Waldo Emerson

"What lies behind us and what lies before us are tiny matters compared to what lies within us."

Ralph Waldo Emerson

"Life is a series of experiences, each one of which makes us bigger, even though sometimes it is hard to realize this. For the world was built to develop character, and we must learn that the setbacks and griefs which we endure help us in our marching onward."

Henry Ford

"Character is not made in a crisis it is only exhibited."

Robert Freeman

"A "No" uttered from deepest conviction is better and greater than a "Yes" merely uttered to please, or what is worse, to avoid trouble."

Mahatma Gandhi

"One man cannot do right in one department of life whilst he is occupied in doing wrong in any other department. Life is one indivisible whole."

Mahatma Gandhi

"Faced with crisis, the man of character falls back on himself. He imposes his own stamp of action, takes responsibility for it, makes it his own."

Charles DeGaulle

"Success is always temporary. When all is said and done, the only thing you'll have left is your character."

Vince Gill

"Talent develops in tranquility, character in the full current of human life."

Johann von Goethe

"A reputation once broken may possibly be repaired, but the world will always keep their eyes on the spot where the crack was."

Joseph Hall

"A good name is seldom regained. When character is gone, all is gone, and one of the richest jewels of life is lost forever."

J. Hawes

"A good character is, in all cases, the fruit of personal exertion. It is not inherited from parents; it is not created by external advantages; it is no necessary appendage of birth, wealth, talents, or station; but it is the result of one's own endeavors-the fruit and reward of good principles manifested in a course of virtuous and honorable action."

J. Hawes

"Character is the result of two things: mental attitude and the way we spend our time."

Elbert Hubbard

"In matters of style swim with the current; In matters of principle, stand like a rock."

Thomas Jefferson

"The true measure of a man is how he treats someone who can do him absolutely no good."

Ann Landers

"What you see and hear depends a great deal on where you are standing; it also depends on what sort of person you are."

C.S. Lewis

"Character is like a tree and reputation its shadow. The shadow is what we think it is; the tree is the real thing."

Abraham Lincoln

"Nearly all men can stand adversity, but if you want to test a man's character, give him power."

Abraham Lincoln

"Things turn out best for the people who make the best of the way things turn out."

Art Linkletter

"A big man is one who makes us feel bigger when we are with him."

John C. Maxwell

"A man's reaction to his appetites and impulses when they are roused gives the measure of that man's character. In these reactions are revealed the man's power to govern or his forced servility to yield."

David O. MacKay

"There is [a] spiritual strength derived from the subjecting of the physical appetite to the will of the individual. "He who reigns within himself and rules passions, desires, and fears is more than king." If there were no other virtues in fasting but gaining strength of character, that alone would be sufficient justification for its universal acceptance."

David O. MacKay

"Character consists of what you do on the third and fourth tries."

James Michener

"A person's treatment of money is the most decisive test of his character, how they make it and how they spend it."

James Moffatt

"The most vital test of a man's character is not how he behaves after success, but how he sustains defeat."

Raymond Moley

"No man can climb out beyond the limitations of his own character."

John Lord Morley

"Character is a subtle thing. Its sources are obscure, its roots delicate and invisible. We know it when we see it and it always commands our admiration, and the absence of it our pity; but it is largely a matter of will."

Leo J. Muir

"Not a day passes over the earth, but men and women of no note do great deeds, speak great words and suffer noble sorrows."

Charles Reade

"Calamity is the test of integrity."

Samuel Richardson

"I believe in the sacredness of a promise, that a man's word should be as good as his bond; that character - not wealth or power or position - is of supreme worth."

John (Jay) Davison Rockefeller, IV

"Live in such a way that you would not be ashamed to sell your parrot to the town gossip."

Will Rogers

"Character, in the long run, is the decisive factor in the life of an individual and of nations alike."

Theodore Roosevelt

"Character is the foundation stone upon which one must build to win respect. Just as no worthy building can be erected on a weak foundation, so no lasting reputation worthy of respect can be built on a weak character."

R.C. Samsel

"It is easy to be tolerant of the principles of other people if you have none of your own."

Herbert Samuel

"Be more concerned with your character than with your reputation. Your character is what you really are, while your reputation is merely what others think you are."

John Wooden

"Show me a man who cannot bother to do little things and I'll show you a man who cannot be trusted to do big things."

Lawrence Bell

"The time is always right to do what is right."

Martin Luther King Jr.

"The ultimate measure of a man is not where he stands in moments of comfort and convenience but where he stands at times of challenge."

Martin Luther King Jr.

"I believe that every right implies a responsibility; every opportunity, an obligation; every possession, a duty."

John D. Rockefeller

"We make a living by what we get, but we make a life by what we give."

Winston Churchill

"Before you can inspire with emotion, you must be swamped with it yourself. Before you can move their tears, your own must flow. To convince them, you must yourself believe."

Winston Churchill

"Quiet minds cannot be perplexed or frightened, but go on in fortune or misfortune at their own private pace, like a clock during a thunderstorm."

Robert Louis Stevenson

"He that can heroically endure adversity will bear prosperity with equal greatness of soul; for the mind that cannot be dejected by the former is not likely to be transported with the latter."

Henry Fielding

"Keep true, never be ashamed of doing right, decide on what you think is right and stick to it."

George Eliot

"It requires a strong constitution to withstand repeated attacks of prosperity."

J. L. Basford

"For a hundred that can bear adversity there is hardly one that can bear prosperity."

Thomas Carlyle

"When you have a number of disagreeable duties to perform, always do the most disagreeable first."

Josiah Quincy

Debt

"Debt is a willing servant but a cruel master."

Ezra Taft Benson

"If there is any one thing that will bring peace and contentment into the human heart and into the family, it is to live within our means, and if there is any one thing that is grinding and discouraging and disheartening, it is to have debts and obligations that one cannot meet."

Heber J. Grant

"Interest never sleeps nor sickens nor dies; it never goes to the hospital; it works on Sunday's and holidays; it never takes a vacation; it never visits nor travels; it takes no pleasure; it is never laid off work nor discharged from employment; it never works on reduced hours; it never has short crops nor droughts; it never pays taxes; it buys no food; it wears no clothes; it is unhoused and without home and so has no repairs, no replacements, no shingling, plumbing, painting, or whitewashing; it has neither wife, children, father, mother, nor kinfolk to watch over and care for; it has no expense of living; it has neither weddings nor births nor deaths; it has no love, no sympathy; it is as hard and soulless as a granite cliff. Once in debt, interest is your companion every minute of the day and night; you cannot shun it or slip away from it; you cannot dismiss it; it yields neither to entreaties, demands, or orders; and whenever you get in its way or cross its course or fail to meet its demands, it crushes you."

J. Reuben Clark, Jr.

Determination

"When nothing seems to help, I go and look at a stonecutter hammering away at his rock perhaps a hundred times without as much as a crack showing in it. Yet at the hundred and first blow it will split in two, and I know it was not that blow that did it - but all that had gone before."

Jacob Riis

"Confronting and overcoming challenges is an exhilarating experience. It does something to feed the soul and the mind. It makes you more than you were before. It strengthens the mental muscles and enables you to become better prepared for the next challenge."

Jim Rohn

"The man who can drive himself further once the effort gets painful is the man who will win."

Roger Bannister

"Show me someone who has done something worthwhile, and I'll show you someone who has overcome adversity."

Lou Holtz

"The spirit, the will to win, and the will to excel are the things that endure. These qualities are so much more important than the events that occur."

Vince Lombardi

"The difference between the impossible and the possible lies in a person's determination."

Tommy Lasorda

"Nothing great will ever be achieved without great men, and men are great only if they are determined to be so."

Charles De Gaulle

"If your determination is fixed, I do not counsel you to despair. Few things are impossible to diligence and skill. Great works are performed not by strength, but perseverance."

Samuel Johnson

"What this power is I cannot say; all I know is that it exists and it becomes available only when a man is in that state of mind in which he knows exactly what he wants and is fully determined not to quit until he finds it."

Alexander Graham Bell

"Nothing can resist the human will that will stake even its existence on its stated purpose."

Benjamin Disraeli

"The longer I live, the more I am certain that the great difference between the great and the insignificant, its energy - invincible determination - a purpose once fixed, and then death or victory."

Sir Thomas Fowell Buxton

"You can do what you have to do, and sometimes you can do it even better than you think you can."

Jimmy Carter

"A determined soul will do more with a rusty monkey wrench than a loafer will accomplish with all the tools in a machine shop."

Robert Hughes

"Every worthwhile accomplishment, big or little, has its stages of drudgery and triumph; a beginning, a struggle and a victory."

Mahatma Gandhi

"Bear in mind, if you are going to amount to anything, that your success does not depend upon the brilliancy and the impetuosity with which you take hold, but upon the everlasting and sanctified bull-doggedness with which you hang on after you have taken hold."

Dr. A. B. Meldrum

"Instead of crying over spilt milk, go milk another cow."

Erna Asp

"The price of success is hard work, dedication to the job at hand, and the determination that whether we win or lose, we have applied the best of ourselves to the task at hand."

Vince Lombardi

"The only good luck many great men ever had was being born with the ability and determination to overcome bad luck."

Channing Pollock

"Success is just a matter of luck-just ask any failure."

Zig Ziglar

"Obstacles don't have to stop you. If you run into a wall, don't turn around and give up. Figure out how to climb it, go through it, or work around it."

Michael Jordon

"Nothing in the world can take the place of persistence. Talent will not; nothing is more common than unsuccessful men with talent. Genius will not; unrewarded genius is almost a proverb. Education alone will not; the world is full of educated derelicts. Persistence and determination alone are omnipotent. The slogan "press on" has solved and always will solve the problems of the human race."

Calvin Coolidge

"I am not discouraged, because every wrong attempt discarded is another step forward."

Thomas Edison

"No, I never did get lost, but I was bewildered for three days once."

Daniel Boone

"We will either find a way or make one."

Hannibal

"Decision and determination are the engineer and fireman of our train to opportunity and success."

Burt Lawlor

"It's a very funny thing about life; if you refuse to accept anything but the best, you very often get it."

William Somerset Maugham

"A resolute determination is the truest wisdom."

Napoléon I

"Determination is the wake-up call to the human will."

Anthony Robbins

"It was courage, faith, endurance and a dogged determination to surmount all obstacles that built this bridge."

John J. Watson

"I learned about the strength you can get from a close family life. I learned to keep going, even in bad times. I learned not to despair, even when my world was falling apart. I learned that there are no free lunches. And I learned the value of hard work."

Lee Iacocca

"A leader, once convinced that a particular course of action is the right one, must....be undaunted when the going gets tough."

Ronald Reagan

"The man who is swimming against the stream knows the strength of it."

Woodrow Wilson

"Fight one more round. When your arms are so tired that you can hardly lift your hands to come on guard, fight one more round. When your nose is bleeding and your eyes are black and you are so tired that you wish your opponent would crack you one on the jaw and put you to sleep, fight one more round - remembering that the man who always fights one more round is never whipped."

James Corbett

"He who has a why to live for can bear almost any how."

Friedrich Nietzsche

"The ripest peach is highest on the tree."

James Whitcomb Riley

Discipline

"You never will be the person you can be if pressure, tension and discipline are taken out of your life."
Dr. James G. Bilkey

"In reading the lives of great men, I found that the first victory they won was over themselves... self-discipline with all of them came first."
Harry S. Truman

"The ability to make yourself do what you should do, when you should do it, whether you feel like it or not."
Elbert Hubbard

"It is better to conquer yourself than to win a thousand battles. Then the victory is yours. It cannot be taken from you, not by angels or by demons, heaven or hell."
Buddha

"The first and the best victory is to conquer self."
Plato

"First we form habits, then they form us. Conquer your bad habits or they will conquer you."
Rob Gilbert

"No man or woman has achieved an effective personality who is not self-disciplined. Such discipline must not be an end in itself, but must be directed to the development of resolute Christian character."

John S. Bonnell

"If you do not conquer self, you will be conquered by self."

Napoleon Hill

"Discipline yourself to do the things you need to do when you need to do them, and the day will come when you will be able to do the things you want to do when you want to do them!"

Zig Ziglar

"The chief cause of failure and unhappiness is trading what you want most for what you want now."

Zig Ziglar

"No horse gets anywhere until he is harnessed. No stream or gas drives anything until it is confined. No Niagara is ever turned into light and power until it is tunneled. No life ever grows great until it is focused, dedicated, disciplined."

Harry Emerson Fosdick

"The only discipline that lasts is self-discipline."

Bum Phillips

"Nothing of importance is ever achieved without discipline. I feel myself sometimes not wholly in sympathy with some modern educational theorists, because I think that they underestimate the part that discipline plays. But the discipline you have in your life should be one determined by your own desires and your own needs, not put upon you by society or authority."

Bertrand Russell

"If we conducted ourselves as sensibly in good times as we do in hard times, we could all acquire a competence."

William Feather

"Men are anxious to improve their circumstances, but are unwilling to improve themselves; they therefore remain bound. The man who does not shrink from self-crucifixion can never fail to accomplish the object upon which his heart is set. This is true of earthly as of heavenly things. Even the man whose object is to acquire wealth must be prepared to make great personal sacrifices before he can accomplish his object; and how much more so he who would realize a strong and well-poised life."

James Allen

"Discipline is remembering what you want."

David Campbell

"If we don't discipline ourselves, the world will do it for us."

William Feather

"The hope of a secure and livable world lies with disciplined nonconformists who are dedicated to justice, peace and brotherhood."

Martin Luther King Jr.

"It is one of the strange ironies of this strange life that those who work the hardest, who subject themselves to the strictest discipline, who give up certain pleasurable things in order to achieve a goal, are the happiest men. When you see 20 or 30 men line up for a distance race in some meet, don't pity them, don't feel sorry for them. Better envy them instead."

Brutus Hamilton

"To discipline ourselves through fasting brings us in tune with God, and fast day provides an occasion to set aside the temporal so that we might enjoy the higher qualities of the spiritual. As we fast on that day we learn and better understand the needs of those who are less fortunate."

Howard W. Hunter

"Discipline is the bridge between goals and accomplishments."

Jim Rohn

"I forget who it was that recommended men for their soul's good to do each day two things they disliked. . . . It is a precept I have followed scrupulously: for every day I have got up and I have gone to bed."

William Somerset Maugham

"Man can learn self-discipline without becoming ascetic; he can be wise without waiting to be old; he can be influential without waiting for status. Man can sharpen his ability to distinguish between matters of principle and matters of preference, but only if we have a wise interplay between time and truth, between minutes and morality."

Neal A. Maxwell

"Discipline is the soul of an army. It makes small numbers formidable, procures success to the weak, and esteem to all."

George Washington

"Nothing is more harmful to the service, than the neglect of discipline; for that discipline, more than numbers, gives one army superiority over another."

George Washington

"One-half of life is luck; the other half is discipline – and that's the important half, for without discipline you wouldn't know what to do with luck."

Carl Zuckmeyer

"The time is always right to do what is right."
Martin Luther King Jr.

"Develop the winning edge; small differences in your performance can lead to large differences in your results."
Brian Tracy

"I learned about the strength you can get from a close family life. I learned to keep going, even in bad times. I learned not to despair, even when my world was falling apart. I learned that there are no free lunches. And I learned the value of hard work."
Lee Iacocca

"Your own mind is a sacred enclosure into which nothing harmful can enter except by your promotion."
Ralph Waldo Emerson

"One discipline always leads to another discipline."
Jim Rohn

"When you have a number of disagreeable duties to perform, always do the most disagreeable first."
Josiah Quincy

"Everyone thinks of changing the world, but no one thinks of changing himself."
Leo Tolstoy

"The successful person has the habit of doing the things failures don't like to do. They don't like doing them either necessarily. But their disliking is subordinated to the strength of their purpose."

E.M. Gray

"I count him braver who overcomes his desires than him who conquers his enemies; for the hardest victory is over self."

Aristotle

Dreams

"Dream no small dreams for they have no power to move the hearts of men."

Johann von Goethe

"I don't dream at night, I dream all day; I dream for a living."

Steven Spielberg

"Make no little plans, they have no magic to stir men's blood and will not be realized. Make big plans; aim high in hope and work, remembering that a noble and logical plan never dies, but long after we are gone will be a living thing."

Lita Bane

"Vision without action is merely a dream. Action without vision just passes the time. Vision with action can change the world."

Joel Barker

"Cherish your visions and your dreams, as they are the children of your soul; the blueprints of your ultimate achievements."

Napoleon Hill

"Man, alone, has the power to transform his thoughts into physical reality; man, alone, can dream and make his dreams come true."

Napoleon Hill

"There is nothing like a dream to create the future."

Victor Hugo

"Hold fast to dreams for if dreams die, life is a broken-winged bird that cannot fly."

Langston Hughes

"It may be that those who do most, dream most."

Stephen Butler Leacock

"The future belongs to those who believe in the beauty of their dreams."

Eleanor Roosevelt

"Dream lofty dreams, and as you dream, so shall you become. Your vision is the promise of what you shall at last unveil."

John Ruskin

"Go confidently in the direction of your dreams. Live the life you've imagined."

Henry David Thoreau

"If one advances confidently in the direction of his dreams, and endeavors to live the life which he has imagined, he will meet with a success unexpected in common hours."

Henry David Thoreau

"We should show life neither as it is nor as it ought to be, but only as we see it in our dreams."

Leo Tolstoy

"It takes a lot of courage to show your dreams to someone else."

Erma Bombeck

"We grow great by dreams. All big men are dreamers. They see things in the soft haze of a spring day or in the red fire of a long winter's evening. Some of us let these great dreams die, but others nourish and protect them; nurse them through bad days till they bring them to the sunshine and light which comes always to those who sincerely hope that their dreams will come true."

Woodrow Wilson

"The great pleasure in life is doing what people say you cannot do."

Walter Bagehot

"The indispensable first step to getting the things you want out of life is this: decide what you want."

Ben Stein

"Lord, grant that I may always desire more than I can accomplish."

Michelangelo

Failure

"I have missed more than 9000 shots in my career. I have lost almost 300 games. On 26 occasions I have been entrusted to take the game winning shot . . . and missed. And I have failed over and over and over again in my life. And that is why . . . I succeed."

Michael Jordan

"Failure should be our teacher, not our undertaker. Failure is delay, not defeat. It is a temporary detour, not a dead end. Failure is something we can avoid only by saying nothing, doing nothing, and being nothing."

Denis Waitley

"You don't drown by falling in water; you only drown if you stay there."

Zig Ziglar

"Failure is an event, not a person. Yesterday ended last night."

Zig Ziglar

"The price of success is much lower than the price of failure."

Zig Ziglar

"When one door closes another door opens; but we often look so long and so regretfully upon the closed door, that we do not see the ones which open for us."

Alexander Graham Bell

"Failure is the opportunity to begin again more intelligently."

Henry Ford

"The men who have done big things are those who were not afraid to attempt big things, who were not afraid to risk failure in order to gain success."

B.C. Forbes

"Someday I hope to enjoy enough of what the world calls success so that someone will ask me, "What's the secret of it?" I shall say simply this: 'I get up when I fall down.'"

Paul Harvey

"Most successful people can identify one minute, one moment, where their lives changed, and it usually occurred in times of adversity."

Willie Jolley

"I think everyone should experience defeat at least once during their career. You learn a lot from it."

Lou Holtz

"When you are down on your back, if you can look up, you can get up."

Les Brown

"There are no failures - only feedback."

R. Bandler

"Failure is the path of least resistance."

James M. Barrie

"If at first you don't succeed, think how many people you've made happy."

H. Duane Black

"Don't fear failure so much that you refuse to try new things. The saddest summary of a life contains three descriptions: could have, might have, and should have."

Louis E. Boone

"A minute's success pays the failure for years."

Robert Browning

"I'd rather be a failure in something that I love than a success in something that I hate."

George Burns

"A man may fail many times, but he isn't a failure until he begins to blame somebody else."

John Burroughs

"Men are failures, not because they are stupid, but
because they are not sufficiently impassioned."
Struther Burt

"Failure is the condiment that gives success its flavor."
Truman Capote

"Show me someone content with mediocrity and I'll
show you someone destined for failure."
Johnetta Cole

"In order to succeed you must fail, so that you know
what not to do the next time."
Anthony D'Angelo

"The only real failure in life is one not learned from."
Anthony D'Angelo

"Defeat never comes to any man until he admits it."
Josephus Daniels

"The person who really thinks learns quite as much
from his failures as from his successes."
John Dewey

"Show me a thoroughly satisfied man, and I will show
you a failure."
Thomas Edison

"Life is a grindstone; whether it grinds you down or polishes you up depends on what you're made of."

Jacob M. Braude

"I'm proof against that word failure. I've seen behind it. The only failure a man ought to fear is failure of cleaving to the purpose he sees to be best."

George Elliot

"The great dividing line between success and failure can be expressed in five words: "I did not have time."

Franklin Field

"Keep these concepts in mind: You've failed many times, although you don't remember. You fell down the first time you tried to walk. You almost drowned the first time you tried to swim. . . . Don't worry about failure. My suggestion to each of you: Worry about the chances you miss when you don't even try."

Sherman Finesilver

"Failure is success if we learn from it."

Malcolm Forbes

"A shy failure is nobler than an immodest success."

Kahlil Gibran

"Haste in every business brings failure."

Herodotus

"Before success comes in any man's life he is sure to meet with much temporary defeat and, perhaps, some failures. When defeat overtakes a man, the easiest and most logical thing to do is to quit. That is exactly what the majority of men do."

Napoleon Hill

"No man is ever whipped, until he quits -- in his own mind."

Napoleon Hill

"Persistence is to the character of man as carbon is to steel."

Napoleon Hill

"The majority of men meet with failure because of their lack of persistence in creating new plans to take the place of those which fail."

Napoleon Hill

"When defeat comes, accept it as a signal that your plans are not sound, rebuild those plans, and set sail once more toward your coveted goal."

Napoleon Hill

"There is no loneliness greater than the loneliness of a failure. The failure is a stranger in his own house."

Eric Hoffer

"When on the brink of complete discouragement, success is discerning that . . . the line between failure and success is so fine that often a single extra effort is all that is needed to bring victory out of defeat."

Elbert Hubbard

"There is no failure except in no longer trying. There is no defeat except from within, no really insurmountable barrier save our own inherent weakness of purpose."

Frank "Kin" Hubbard

"An inventor fails 999 times, and if he succeeds once, he's in. He treats his failures simply as practice shots."

Charles Kettering

"Failure is the foundation of success, and the means by which it is achieved."

Lao-Tze

"My great concern is not whether you have failed, but whether you are content with your failure."

Abraham Lincoln

"The probability that we may fail in struggle ought not to deter us from the support of a cause we believe to be just"

Abraham Lincoln

"In great attempts it is glorious even to fail."

Vince Lombardi

"What we call failure is not the falling down, but the staying down."

Mary Pickford

"Because a fellow has failed once or twice, or a dozen times, you don't want to set him down as a failure till he's dead or loses his courage - and that's the same thing."

George Horace Lorimer

"Remember the two benefits of failure. First, if you do fail, you learn what doesn't work; and second, the failure gives you the opportunity to try a new approach."

Roger Von Oech

"If we don't succeed, we run the risk of failure."

Dan Quayle

"I've come to believe that all my past failure and frustrations were actually laying the foundation for the understandings that have created the new level of living I now enjoy."

Anthony Robbins

"Failure is not a single, cataclysmic event. You don't fail overnight. Instead, failure is a few errors in judgment, repeated every day."

Jim Rohn

"Success is never ending: failure is never final."
Robert Schuller

"When it is dark enough, men see the stars."
Benjamin Disraeli

"You may be disappointed if you fail, but you are doomed if you don't try."
Beverly Sills

"The bravest sight in the world is to see a great man struggling against adversity."
Lucius Annæus Seneca

"I thank God for my handicaps, for through them, I have found myself, my work and my God."
Helen Keller

"The saddest failures in life are those that come from not putting forth the power and will to succeed."
Edwin Percy Welles

"I would rather lose in a cause that I know some day will triumph than to triumph in a cause that I know some day will fail."
Wendell Wilkie

"Defeat is not the worst of failures. Not to have tried is the true failure."

George E. Woodberry

"No one can defeat us unless we first defeat ourselves."

Dwight Eisenhower

"If you think education is expensive, try ignorance."

Derek Bok

"It is not the great temptations that ruin us; it is the little ones."

John W. DeForest

"No one that ever lived has ever had enough power, prestige or knowledge to overcome the basic condition of all life--you win some and you lose some."

Ken Keyes

Focus

"Determine what specific goal you want to achieve. Then dedicate yourself to its attainment with unswerving singleness of purpose, the trenchant zeal of a crusader."

Paul J. Meyer

"You will become as great as your dominant aspiration. If you cherish a vision, a lofty ideal in your heart, you will realize it."

James Allen

"There is one quality which one must possess to win, and that is definiteness of purpose, the knowledge of what one wants and a burning desire to possess it."

Ronald Reagan

"The human mind is not rich enough to drive many horses abreast and wants one general scheme, under which it strives to bring everything."

George Santayana

"The successful woman is the average woman-- focused."

Ruth Williams

"Nothing focuses the mind better than the constant sight of a competitor who wants to wipe you off the map."

Wayne Calloway

"There are two ways to look at life and the world. We can see the good or the bad, the beautiful or the ugly. Both are there, and what we focus on and choose to see is what brings us feelings of joy or feelings of despair."

Lloyd Newell

"Most people have no idea of the giant capacity we can immediately command when we focus all of our resources on mastering a single area of our lives."

Anthony Robbins

"It's not what's happening to you now or what has happened in your past that determines who you become. Rather, it's your decisions about what to focus on, what things mean to you, and what you're going to do about them that will determine your ultimate destiny."

Anthony Robbins

"The successful warrior is the average man, with laser-like focus."

Bruce Lee

"If you focus on results, you will never change. If you focus on change, you will get results."

Jack Dixon

"Do not let what you can't do interfere with what you can do."

John Wooden

"Keep your mind on the things you want and off the things you don't want."

Hannah Whitall Smith

"Visualize this thing you want. See it, feel it, believe in it. Make your mental blueprint and begin."

Robert Collier

Goals

"The person with a fixed goal, a clear picture of his desire, or an ideal always before him, causes it, through repetition, to be buried deeply in his subconscious mind and is thus enabled, thanks to its generative and sustaining power, to realize his goal in a minimum of time and with a minimum of physical effort. Just pursue the thought unceasingly. Step by step you will achieve realization, for all your faculties and powers become directed to that end."

Claude M. Bristol

"There is no achievement without goals."

Robert J. McKaine

"Goals give you more than a reason to get up in the morning; they are an incentive to keep you going all day. Goals tend to tap the deeper resources and draw the best out of life."

Harvey Mackay

"When you develop a game plan to get what you want, you will develop a belief that you can get it."

Zig Ziglar

"What you get by reaching your destination is not nearly as important as what you will become by reaching your destination."

Zig Ziglar

"The basic goal-reaching principle is to understand that you go as far as you can see, and when you get there you will always be able to see farther."

Zig Ziglar

"If you don't have a plan (goals) for what you want, then you will probably find yourself buying into someone else's plan and later find out that wasn't the direction you wanted to go. You've got to be the architect of your life."

Jim Rohn

"Now is the time to fix the next ten years."

Jim Rohn

"This one step - choosing a goal and sticking to it – changes everything."

Scott Reed

"People with goals succeed because they know where they're going."

Earl Nightingale

"Until input (thought) is linked to a goal (purpose) there can be no intelligent accomplishment."

Paul G. Thomas

"Without goals, and plans to reach them, you are like a ship that has set sail with no destination."

Fitzhugh Dodson

"Goals. There's no telling what you can do when you get inspired by them. There's no telling what you can do when you believe in them. There's no telling what will happen when you act upon them."

Jim Rohn

"Aim for the top. There is plenty of room there. There are so few at the top it is almost lonely there."

Samuel Insull

"The goal you set must be challenging. At the same time, it should be realistic and attainable, not impossible to reach. It should be challenging enough to make you stretch, but not so far that you break."

Rick Hansen

"You must have long term goals to keep you from being frustrated by short term failures."

Charles C. Noble

"What you get by achieving your goals is not as important as what you become by achieving your goals."

Zig Ziglar

"First say to yourself what you would be; and then do what you have to do."

Epictetus

"If you don't know where you are going, you might wind up someplace else."

Yogi Berra

"Go for the moon. If you don't get it, you'll still be heading for a star."

Willis Reed

"It is those who concentrate on but one thing at a time who advance in this world."

Og Mandino

"Our goals can only be reached through a vehicle of a plan, in which we must fervently believe, and upon which we must vigorously act. There is no other route to success."

Stephen A. Brennan

"If I've got correct goals, and if I keep pursuing them the best way I know how, everything falls into line. If I do the right thing right, I'm going to succeed."

Dan Dierdorf

"If you raise your children to feel that they can accomplish any goal or task they decide upon, you will have succeeded as a parent and you will have given your children the greatest of all blessings."

Brian Tracy

"We aim above the mark to hit the mark."

Ralph Waldo Emerson

"It is for us to pray not for tasks equal to our powers, but for powers equal to our tasks, to go forward with a great desire forever beating at the door of our hearts as we travel toward our distant goal."

Helen Keller

"Difficulties increase the nearer we approach the goal."

Johann Von Goethe

"From a certain point onward there is no longer any turning back. That is the point that must be reached."

Franz Kafka

"Decide what you want, decide what you are willing to exchange for it. Establish your priorities and go to work."

H. L. Hunt

"Nothing can add more power to your life than concentrating all your energies on a limited set of targets."

Nido Qubein

"Nothing can stop the man with the right mental attitude from achieving his goal; nothing on earth can help the man with the wrong mental attitude."

Thomas Jefferson

"Begin with the end in mind."

Stephen Covey

"My philosophy of life is that if we make up our mind what we are going to make of our lives, then work hard toward that goal, we never lose - somehow we win out."

Ronald Reagan

"Having an exciting destination is like setting a needle in your compass. From then on, the compass knows only one point-its ideal. And it will faithfully guide you there through the darkest nights and fiercest storms."

Daniel Boone

"By recording your dreams and goals on paper, you set in motion the process of becoming the person you most want to be."

Mark Victor Hansen

"Nothing is too high for a man to reach, but he must climb with care and confidence."

Hans Christian Andersen

"What this power is I cannot say; all I know is that it exists and it becomes available only when a man is in that state of mind in which he knows exactly what he wants and is fully determined not to quit until he finds it."

Alexander Graham Bell

"A man's reach should exceed his grasp, or what's heaven for?"

Robert Browning

"When a great man has some one object in view to be achieved in a given time, it may be absolutely necessary for him to walk out of all the common roads."

Edmund Burke

"Define your business goals clearly so that others can see them as you do."

George F. Burns

"Desires must be simple and definite. They defeat their own purpose should they be too many, too confusing, or beyond a man's training to accomplish."

George Clason

"Hitch your wagon to a star."

Ralph Waldo Emerson

"Keep your eye on eternal goals."

John H. Groberg

"Success is not measured in achievement of goals, but in the stress and strain of meeting those goals."

Spencer W. Kimball

"Never look down to test the ground before taking your next step; only he who keeps his eye fixed on the far horizon will find the right road."

Dag Hammarskjöld

"There is one quality which one must possess to win, and that is definiteness of purpose, the knowledge of what one wants, and a burning desire to possess it."

Napoleon Hill

"Please don't nag yourself with thoughts of failure. Do not set goals far beyond your capacity to achieve. Simply do what you can do, in the best way you know, and the Lord will accept of your effort."

Gordon B. Hinckley

"You can't hit a home run unless you step up to the plate. You can't catch fish unless you put your line in the water. You can't reach your goals if you don't try."

Kathy Seligman

"Go as far as you can see, and when you get there you will see farther."

Orison Swett Marden

"Do not let the future be held hostage by the past."

Neal A. Maxwell

"We all need lots of powerful long-range goals to help us past the short-term obstacles.

Jim Rohn

"When a man does not know what harbor he is making for, no wind is the right wind."

Lucius Annæus Seneca

"We do believe in setting goals. We live by goals. In athletics we always have a goal. When we go to school, we have the goal of graduation and degrees. Our total existence is goal-oriented. We must have goals to make progress, encouraged by keeping records . . . as the swimmer or the jumper or the runner does . . . Progress is easier when it is timed, checked, and measured. . . .Goals are good. Laboring with a distant aim sets the mind in a higher key and puts us at our best. Goals should always be made to a point that will make us reach and strain."

Spencer W. Kimball

"Our strength lies, not alone in our proving grounds and our stockpiles, but in our ideals, our goals, and their universal appeal to all men who are struggling to breathe free."

Adlai Stevenson

"To solve a problem or to reach a goal, you...don't need to know all the answers in advance. But you must have a clear idea of the problem or the goal you want to reach."

W. Clement Stone

"You, too, can determine what you want. You can decide on your major objectives, targets, aims and destination."

W. Clement Stone

"If one advances confidently in the direction of his own dreams and endeavors to live the life which he has imagined, he will meet with a success unexpected in common hours.

Henry David Thoreau

"In the long run men hit only what they aim at."

Henry David Thoreau

"One ship drives east, and another west
With the self-same winds that blow:
'Tis the set of the sails
And not the gales,
Which decides the way we go.
Like the winds of the sea are the ways of fate,
As they voyage along through life;
'Tis the will of the soul
That decides its goal,
And not the calm or the strife."

Ella Wheeler Wilcox

"There is no chance, no destiny, no fate,
That can circumvent or hinder or control
The firm resolve of a determined soul."

Ella Wheeler Wilcox

"You can't hit a target you cannot see, and you cannot see a target you do not have."

Zig Ziglar

"We must walk consciously only part way toward our goal and then leap in the dark to our success."

Henry David Thoreau

"Men do not succeed in business or in life, no matter how intelligent they may be, no matter how sharply their aptitudes are defined, no matter how brilliantly they may be educated unless they are oriented toward the proper goals and have the drive or motivating force to succeed. One has to want something mighty hard and keep on wanting things all his life. . . ."

Wallace H. Wulfeck

"If you have built castles in the air, your work need not be lost; that is where they should be. Now put the foundations under them."

Henry David Thoreau

"Reduce your plan to writing... The moment you complete this, you will have definitely given concrete form to the intangible desire."

Napoleon Hill

"Make no little plans; they have no magic to stir men's blood. Make big plans, aim high in hope and work."

Daniel H. Burnham

"In the long run men hit only what they aim at.
Therefore, though they should fail immediately, they had
better aim at something high."

Henry David Thoreau

"Desire is the key to motivation, but it's the
determination and commitment to an unrelenting pursuit
of your goal - a commitment to excellence - that will
enable you to attain the success you seek."

Mario Andretti

Greatness

"Great men are true men, the men in whom nature has succeeded. They are not extraordinary - they are in the true order. It is the other species of men who are not what they ought to be."
Henri Frederic Amiel

"Creativity means believing you have greatness."
Dr. Wayne W. Dyer

"There are no great men, only great challenges that ordinary men are forced by circumstances to meet."
William F. Halsey

"I shall not remain insignificant, I shall work in the world for mankind....I don't want to have lived in vain like most people. I want to be useful or bring enjoyment to all people, even those I've never met. I want to go on living, even after my death!"
Anne Frank

"A man, as a general rule, owes very little to what he is born with – a man is what he makes himself."
Alexander Graham Bell

"Time and money spent in helping men do more for themselves is far better than mere giving."

Henry Ford

"No great man ever complains of want of opportunity."

Ralph Waldo Emerson

"Be not afraid of greatness; some are born great, some achieve greatness, and others have greatness thrust upon them."

William Shakespeare

"No great man lives in vain. The history of the world is but the biography of great men."

Thomas Carlyle

"Man is only truly great when he acts from his passions."

Benjamin Disraeli

"Great men are like eagles, and build their nest on some lofty solitude."

Arthur Schopenhauer

"The price of greatness is responsibility."

Winston Churchill

"I can't believe that God put us on this earth to be ordinary."

Lou Holtz

"The ultimate is not to win, but to reach within the depths of your capabilities and to compete against yourself."

Billy Mills

"It is the privilege of posterity to set matters right between those antagonists who, by their rivalry for greatness, divided a whole age."

Joseph Addison

"Every great man is unique."

Ralph Waldo Emerson

"Greatness after all, in spite of its name, appears to be not so much a certain size as a certain quality in human lives. It may be present in lives whose range is very small."

Phillips Brooks

"Is it so bad, then, to be misunderstood? Pythagoras was misunderstood, and Socrates, and Jesus, and Luther, and Copernicus, and Galileo, and Newton, and every pure and wise spirit that ever took flesh. To be great is to be misunderstood."

Ralph Waldo Emerson

"To be great is to be misunderstood."

Ralph Waldo Emerson

"Whenever you see a successful business, someone once made a courageous decision."

Peter Drucker

"Do not confuse notoriety and fame with greatness. . . . For you see, greatness is a measure of one's spirit, not a result of one's rank in human affairs."

Sherman Finesilver

"Let us consider the nature of true greatness in men. The people who can catch hold of men's minds and feelings and inspire them to do things bigger than themselves are the people who are remembered in history. . . . those who stir feelings and imagination and make men struggle toward perfection."

Henry Eyring

"A great man will not trample upon a worm, nor sneak to an emperor."

Thomas Fuller

"A desire for bigness has hurt many folks. Putting oneself in the limelight at the expense of others is a wrong idea of greatness. The secret of greatness rather than bigness is to acclimate oneself to one's place of service and be true to one's own convictions. A life of this kind of service will forever remain the measure of one's true greatness."

Richard W. Shelly, Jr.

"When you cannot make up your mind which of two evenly balanced courses of action you should take—choose the bolder."

W. J. Slim

"Recipe for greatness - To bear up under loss, to fight the bitterness of defeat and the weakness of grief, to be victor over anger, to smile when tears are close, to resist evil men and base instincts, to hate hate and to love love, to go on when it would seem good to die, to seek ever after the glory and the dream, to look up with unquenchable faith in something evermore about to be, that is what any man can do, and so be great."

Zane Grey

" . . . I want it said of me by those who knew me best, that I always plucked a thistle and planted a flower where I thought a flower would grow."

Abraham Lincoln

"If any man seeks for greatness, let him forget greatness and ask for truth, and he will find both."

Horace Mann

"Every great man is always being helped by everybody, for his gift is to get good out of all things and all persons."

John Ruskin

"You are not here merely to make a living. You are here in order to enable the world to live more amply, with greater vision, with a finer spirit of hope and achievement. You are here to enrich the world, and you impoverish yourself if you forget the errand."

Woodrow Wilson

"Some things have not changed since the dawn of history, and bid fair to last out time itself. One of these things is the capacity for greatness in man-his capacity for being often the master of the event -and sometimes even more-the changer of the course of history itself. This capacity for greatness is a very precious gift, and we are under a danger in our day of stifling it."

Dr. William Clyde de Vane

"Excellence is not a destination; it is a continuous journey that never ends."

Brian Tracy

"You can do anything you wish to do, have anything you wish to have, be anything you wish to be."

Robert Collier

"Since most of us spend our lives doing ordinary tasks, the most important thing is to carry them out extraordinarily well."

Henry David Thoreau

"We make a living by what we get, but we make a life by what we give."

Winston Churchill

"What lies behind us and what lies before us are small matters compared to what lies within us."

Ralph Waldo Emerson

"Great minds discuss ideas, average minds discuss events, small minds discuss people."

Hyman Rickover

"Before you can inspire with emotion, you must be swamped with it yourself. Before you can move their tears, your own must flow. To convince them, you must yourself believe."

Winston Churchill

"Great crises produce great men and great deeds of courage."

John F. Kennedy

"A ship in harbor is safe, but that is not what ships are built for."

John A. Shedd

"He should sweep streets so well that all the host of heaven and earth will pause to say, 'Here lives a great street-sweeper who did his job well'"

Martin Luther King Jr.

"He who reigns within himself and rules his passions, desires, and fears is more than a king."

John Milton

Habits

"Those who have attained things worth having in this world have worked while others idled, have persevered when others gave up in despair, have practiced early in life the valuable habits of self-denial, industry, and singleness of purpose. As a result, they enjoy in later life the success so often erroneously attributed to good luck."

Grenville Kleiser

"You leave old habits behind by starting out with the thought, 'I release the need for this in my life'."

Dr. Wayne Dyer

"In essence, if we want to direct our lives, we must take control of our consistent actions. It's not what we do once in a while that shapes our lives, but what we do consistently."

Anthony Robbins

"If I feel depressed, I go to work. Work is always an antidote to depression."

Eleanor Roosevelt

"We are what we repeatedly do. Excellence then, is not an act, but a habit."

Aristotle

"A nail is driven out by another nail. Habit is overcome by habit."

Desiderius Erasmus

"First we form habits, then they form us. Conquer your bad habits or they will conquer you."

Rob Gilbert

"Power is the faculty or capacity to act, the strength and potency to accomplish something. It is the vital energy to make choices and decisions. It also includes the capacity to overcome deeply embedded habits and to cultivate higher, more effective ones."

Stephen Covey

"Motivation gets you going and habit gets you there. Make motivation a habit and you will get there more quickly and have more fun on the trip."

Zig Ziglar

"Winning is a habit. Unfortunately, so is losing."

Vince Lombardi

"Your net worth to the world is usually determined by what remains after your bad habits are subtracted from your good ones."

Benjamin Franklin

"Habits... the only reason they persist is that they are offering some satisfaction... You allow them to persist by not seeking any other, better form of satisfying the same needs. Every habit, good or bad, is acquired and learned in the same way - by finding that it is a means of satisfaction."

Juliene Berk

"Once you learn to quit, it becomes a habit."

Vince Lombardi

"Thoughts lead on to purposes; purposes go forth in action; actions form habits; habits decide character; and character fixes our destiny."

Tryon Edwards

"I never could have done what I have done without the habits of punctuality, order, and diligence, without the determination to concentrate myself on one subject at a time."

Charles Dickens

"It is hard to let old beliefs go. They are familiar. We are comfortable with them and have spent years building systems and developing habits that depend on them. Like a man who has worn eyeglasses so long that he forgets he has them on, we forget that the world looks to us the way it does because we have become used to seeing it that way through a particular set of lenses. Today, however, we need new lenses. And we need to throw the old ones away."

Kenich Ohmae

"As a twig is bent the tree inclines."

Virgil

"What a curious phenomenon it is that you can get men to die for the liberty of the world who will not make the little sacrifice that is needed to free themselves from their own individual bondage."

Bruce Barton

"1. Be Proactive.
2. Begin with the end in mind.
3. Put first things first.
4. Think win win.
5. Seek first to understand . . . then to be understood.
6. Synergize.
7. Sharpen the saw."

Stephen Covey

"Any act often repeated soon forms a habit; and habit allowed, steadily gains in strength. At first it may be but as the spider's web, easily broken through, but if not resisted it soon binds us with chains of steel."

Tyron Edwards

"The unfortunate thing about this world is that good habits are so much easier to give up than bad ones."

William Somerset Maugham

"A large part of virtue consists in good habits."

Barbara Paley

"The long span of the bridge of your life is supported by countless cables called habits, attitudes, and desires. What you do in life depends upon what you are and what you want. What you get from life depends upon how much you want it-how much you are willing to work and plan and cooperate and use your resources. The long span of the bridge of your life is supported by countless cables that you are spinning now, and that is why today is such an important day. Make the cables strong!"

L.G. Elliott

"We are what we think; as we desire so do we become! By our thoughts, desires, and habits, we either ascend to the full divine dignity of our nature, or we descend to suffer and learn."

J. Todd Ferrier

"We're worn into grooves by Time-by our habits. In the end, these grooves are going to show whether we've been second rate or champions, each in his way in dispatching the affairs of every day. By choosing our habits, we determine the grooves into which Time will wear us; and these are grooves that enrich our lives and make for ease of mind, peace, happiness - achievement."

Frank B. Gilberth

"A habit cannot be tossed out the window; it must be coaxed down the stairs a step at a time."

Mark Twain

"Nothing so needs reforming as other people's habits."
Mark Twain

"No matter how old you get, if you can keep the desire to be creative, you're keeping the man-child alive."
John Cassavetes

"The man who removes a mountain begins by carrying away small stones."
William Faulkner

"Moral excellence comes about as a result of habit. We become just by doing just acts, temperate by doing temperate acts, brave by doing brave acts."
Aristotle

Happiness

"A happy person is not a person in a certain set of circumstances, but rather a person with a certain set of attitudes."

Hugh Downs

"Happiness lies in the joy of achievement and the thrill of creative effort."

Franklin Roosevelt

"The secret of happiness is not in doing what one likes, but in liking what one does."

James M. Barrie

"If you want happiness for an hour - take a nap.
If you want happiness for a day - go fishing.
If you want happiness for a year - inherit a fortune.
If you want happiness for a lifetime - help someone else."

Chinese Proverb

"Happiness is not the result of circumstance. It is the result of loving others."

Lloyd Newell

"Pleasure is not happiness. It has no more importance than a shadow following a man."

Muhammad Ali

"Happiness, it is said, is seldom found by those who seek it, and never by those who seek it for themselves."
F. Emerson Andrews

"Happiness depends upon ourselves."
Aristotle

"Happiness is a state of activity."
Aristotle

"Happiness is a conscious choice, not an automatic response."
Mildred Barthel

"Happiness is like a cat, if you try to coax it or call it, it will avoid you; it will never come. But if you pay not attention to it and go about your business, you'll find it rubbing against your legs and jumping into your lap."
William Bennett

"I remember hearing in a talk that the more we express our gratitude to God for our blessings, the more he will bring to our mind other blessings. The more we are aware of to be grateful for, the happier we become."
Ezra Taft Benson

"…wickedness never was happiness."
The Book of Mormon

"...men are that they might have joy."

The Book of Mormon

"You can make yourself happy or miserable - it's the same amount of effort."

Ray Bradbury

"Happiness quite unshared can scarcely be called happiness; it has no taste."

Charlotte Bronte

"Thousands of candles can be lighted from a single candle, and the life of the candle will not be shortened. Happiness never decreases by being shared."

Buddha

"Your successes and happiness are forgiven you only if you generously consent to share them."

Albert Camus

"Remember happiness doesn't depend upon who you are or what you have; it depends solely on what you think."

Dale Carnegie

"Success is getting what you want; happiness is wanting what you get."

Dale Carnegie

"The grand essentials of happiness are: something to do, something to love, and something to hope for."

Allan K. Chalmers

"The office of government is not to confer happiness, but to give men the opportunity to work out happiness for themselves."

William Channing

"In our daily lives, we must see
That it is not happiness that makes us grateful,
But the gratefulness that makes us happy."

Albert Clarke

"Happiness depends, as Nature shows,
Less on exterior things than most suppose."

William Cowper

"To find out what one is fitted to do and to secure an opportunity to do it is the key to happiness."

John Dewey

"We begin from the recognition that all beings cherish happiness and do not want suffering. It then becomes both morally wrong and pragmatically unwise to pursue only one's own happiness oblivious to the feelings and aspirations of all others who surround us as members of the same human family. The wiser course is to think of others when pursuing our own happiness."

Dalai Lama

"Action may not always bring happiness; but there is no happiness without action."

Benjamin Disraeli

"Be unselfish. That is the first and final commandment for those who would be useful and happy in their usefulness. If you think of yourself only, you cannot develop because you are choking the source of development, which is spiritual expansion through thought for others."

George Eliot

"Happiness is a perfume you cannot pour on others without getting a few drops on yourself."

Ralph Waldo Emerson

"Of cheerfulness, or a good temper - the more it is spent, the more of it remains."

Ralph Waldo Emerson

"It is not by accident that the happiest people are those who make a conscious effort to live useful lives. Their happiness, of course, is not a shallow exhilaration where life is one continuous intoxicating party. Rather, their happiness is a deep sense of inner peace that comes when they believe their lives have meaning and that they are making a difference for good in the world."

Ernest A. Fitzgerald

"How would you know what happy is if you've never been otherwise."

Malcolm Forbes

"There is joy in work. All that money can do is buy us someone else's work in exchange for our own. There is no happiness except in the realization that we have accomplished something."

Henry Ford

"If you would find happiness and joy, lose your life in some noble cause. A worthy purpose must be at the center of every worthy life."

Jack H. Goaslind, Jr.

"Striving for happiness is a long, hard journey with many challenges. It requires eternal vigilance to win the victory. You cannot succeed with sporadic little flashes of effort.
Constant and valiant living is necessary."

Jack H. Goaslind, Jr.

"Whatever mitigates the woes, or increases the happiness of others, is a just criterion of goodness; and whatever injures society at large, or any individual in it, is a criterion of iniquity."

Oliver Goldsmith

"Happiness is not a destination. It is a method of life."

Burton Hills

"Happiness is as a butterfly, which, when pursued, is always beyond our grasp, but which, if you will sit down quietly, may alight upon you."

Nathaniel Hawthorne

"It is one of the strange ironies of this strange life that those who work the hardest, who subject themselves to the strictest discipline, who give up certain pleasurable things in order to achieve a goal, are the happiest men. When you see 20 or 30 men line up for a distance race in some meet, don't pity them, don't feel sorry for them. Better envy them instead."

Brutus Hamilton

"Happiness, in this world, if it comes at all, comes incidentally. Make it the object of pursuit, and it leads us on a wild-goose chase, and it is never attained."

Nathaniel Hawthorne

"The search for happiness is one of the chief sources of unhappiness."

Eric Hoffer

"Love is the master key that opens the gates of happiness."

Oliver Wendell Holmes

"Natural joy brings no headaches and no heartaches."

Elbert Hubbard

"Life's greatest happiness is to be convinced we are loved."

Victor Hugo

"Happiness is not a reward - it is a consequence. Suffering is not a punishment - it is a result."

Robert Green Ingersoll

"True happiness, we are told, consists in getting out of one's self, but the point is not only to get out - you must stay out; and to stay out you must have some absorbing errand."

Henry James Jr.

"Happiness comes of the capacity to feel deeply, to enjoy simply, to think freely, to risk life, to be needed."

Storm Jameson

"It is neither wealth nor splendor, but tranquility and occupation, which give happiness."

Thomas Jefferson

"Labor, if it were not necessary for existence, would be indispensable for the happiness of man."

Samuel Johnson

"It is not necessary that whilst I live I live happily; but it is necessary that so long as I live I should live honorably."

Immanuel Kant

"Many persons have a wrong idea of what constitutes true happiness. It is not attained through self-gratification but through fidelity to a worthy purpose."

Helen Keller

"When one door of happiness closes, another opens; but often we look so long at the closed door that we do not see the one which as been opened for us."

Helen Keller

"Definition of happiness: The full use of your powers along lines of excellence."

John F. Kennedy

"Happiness is something that comes into our lives through doors we don't even remember leaving open."

Rose Lane

"Most people are about as happy as they make up their minds to be."

Abraham Lincoln

"Talk happiness. The world is sad enough without your woe."

Orison Swett Marden

"Happiness is like a kiss. You must share it to enjoy it."

Bernard Melzer

"If you find some happiness inside yourself, you'll start findin' it in lot of other places too."

Gladiola Montana

"Happiness is a matter of one's most ordinary and everyday mode of consciousness being busy and lively and unconcerned with self."

Jean Iris Murdoch

"Happy people plan actions, they don't plan results."

Denis Waitley

"If this world afford true happiness, it is to be found in a home where love and confidence increase with the years, where the necessities of life come without severe strain, where luxuries enter only after their cost has been carefully considered."

Alfred Edward Newton

"The happiness of your life depends upon the quality of your thoughts....take care that you entertain no notions unsuitable to virtue and reasonable nature."

Marcus Aurelius

Health

"Take care of your body. It's the only place you have to live."

Jim Rohn

"Ill-health of body or of mind, is defeat. Health alone is victory. Let all men, if they can manage it, contrive to be healthy!"

Thomas Carlyle

"Treat your body like a temple, not a woodshed. The mind and body work together. Your body needs to be a good support system for the mind and spirit. If you take good care of it, your body can take you wherever you want to go, with the power and strength and energy and vitality you will need to get there."

Jim Rohn

"To get rich never your risk your health. For it is the truth that health is the wealth of wealth."

Richard Baker

"To insure good health: Eat lightly, breathe deeply, live moderately, cultivate cheerfulness, and maintain an interest in life."

William Londen

"A man's health can be judged by which he takes two at a time - pills or stairs."

Joan Welsh

"The sovereign invigorator of the body is exercise, and of all the exercises walking is the best."

Thomas Jefferson

"A man too busy to take care of his health is like a mechanic too busy to take care of his tools."

Spanish Proverb

"He who has health, has hope; and he who has hope, has everything."

Arabian Proverb

"To array a man's will against his sickness is the supreme art of medicine."

Henry Ward Beecher

"Health is the greatest of all possessions; a pale cobbler is better than a sick king."

Isaac Bickerstaff

"The secret of health for both mind and body is not to mourn for the past, not to worry about the future, or not to anticipate troubles, but to live the present moment wisely and earnestly."

Buddha

"The health of the people is really the foundation upon which all their happiness and all their powers as a state depend."

Benjamin Disraeli

"He's the best physician that knows the worthlessness of the most medicines."

Benjamin Franklin

"He who cures a disease may be the skillfullest, but he that prevents it is the safest physician."

Thomas Fuller

"Take care of your body with steadfast fidelity. The soul must see through these eyes alone, and if they are dim, the whole world is clouded."

Johann von Goethe

"A bodily disease which we look upon as whole and entire within itself, may, after all, be but a symptom of some ailment in the spiritual part."

Nathaniel Hawthorne

"Nine-tenths of our sickness can be prevented by right thinking plus right hygiene - nine-tenths of it!"

Henry Miller

"People who laugh actually live longer than those who don't laugh. Few persons realize that health actually varies according to the amount of laughter."

James Walsh

Humorous

"To his dog, every man is Napoleon; hence the constant popularity of dogs."

Aldous Huxley

"I'm so optimistic I'd go after Moby Dick in a row boat and take the tartar sauce with me."

Zig Ziglar

"Some people find fault like there is a reward for it."

Zig Ziglar

"I stay away from natural foods. At my age I need all the preservatives I can get."

George Burns

"Middle age is when your old classmates are so gray and wrinkled and bald they don't recognize you."

Bennett Cerf

"There's one advantage to being 102. There's no peer pressure."

Dennis Wolfberg

"Old age is like everything else, to make a success of it you got to start young."

Fred Astaire

"We learn from experience. A man never wakes up his second baby just to see it smile."

Grace Williams

"Few things are harder to put up with than the annoyance of a good example."

Mark Twain

'Always do right. This will gratify some people, and astonish the rest."

Mark Twain

"Man is the only animal that blushes. Or needs to."

Mark Twain

"In Paris they simply stared when I spoke to them in French; I never did succeed in making those idiots understand their own language."

Mark Twain

"To encourage my little kid to eat I'd sometimes say: 'Just pretend it's sand.'"

Unknown

"Keep in mind…to a dog you are family, to a cat you are staff."

Unknown

"My doctor said I look like a million dollars—green and wrinkled."

Red Skelton

"They say the Japanese don't experience menopause or hot flashes. If that's the case, why are they the number-one fan-producing country in the world?"

Wendy Morgan

"I take my son to McDonald's just to watch him eat and see the numbers change."

Joan Rivers

"I know a man who gave up smoking, drinking, sex, and rich food. He was healthy right up to the time he killed himself."

Johnny Carson

"Men occasionally stumble over the truth, but most of them pick themselves up and hurry off as if nothing happened."

Winston Churchill

"Money doesn't always bring happiness. People with $10 million are no happier than people with $9 million."

Hobart Brown

"The haves and the have-nots can often be traced to the dids and the did-nots."

D. O. Flynn

"The nice thing about being a celebrity is that when you bore people, they think it's their fault."

Henry Kissinger

"I've always wanted to be somebody, but I see now I should have been more specific."

Lily Tomlin

"If your ship doesn't come in, swim out to it."

Jonathan Winters

"Some people see the cup as half empty. Some people see the cup as half full. I see the cup as too large."

George Carlin

"I don't believe in astrology—of course, that's very typical of Leos."

Wendy Morgan

"What a pity human beings can't exchange problems. Everyone knows exactly how to solve the other fellow's."

Olin Miller

Knowledge

"Learning is the beginning of wealth. Learning is the beginning of health. Learning is the beginning of spirituality. Searching and learning is where the miracle process all begins."

Jim Rohn

"Formal education will make you a living. Self-education will make you a fortune."

Jim Rohn

"The highest form of ignorance is to reject something you know nothing about."

Dr. Wayne W. Dyer

"Success means accomplishments as the result of our own efforts and abilities. Proper preparation is the key to our success. Our acts can be no wiser than our thoughts. Our thinking can be no wiser than our understanding."

George Clason

"The more of wisdom we know, the more we may earn. That man who seeks to learn more of his craft shall be richly rewarded."

George Clason

"Nourish the mind like you would your body. The mind cannot survive on junk food."

Jim Rohn

"You are what you are and where you are because of what has gone into your mind. You can change what you are and where you are by changing what goes into your mind."

Zig Ziglar

"Every mind was made for growth, for knowledge, and its nature is sinned against when it is doomed to ignorance."

William Channing

"A good book contains more real wealth than a good bank."

Roy L. Smith

"You are the same today as you will be five years from now except for two things…the people you meet and the books you read."

Charles E. Jones

"Knowledge is power and enthusiasm pulls the switch."
Steve Droke

"Zeal without knowledge is fire without light."
Thomas Fuller

"Today knowledge has power. It controls access to opportunity and advancement."

Peter Drucker

"Not to know is bad; not to wish to know is worse."

African Proverb

"The preservation of the means of knowledge among the lowest ranks is of more importance to the public than all the property of all the rich men in the country."

John Adams

"No matter what his rank or position may be, the lover of books is the richest and happiest of the children of men."

John Alfred Langford

"Many times the reading of a book has made the future of a man."

Ralph Waldo Emerson

"All men by nature desire to know."

Aristotle

"For knowledge, too, is itself power."

Francis Bacon

"Knowledge and human power are synonymous, since the ignorance of the cause frustrates the effect."

Francis Bacon

"Knowledge is a rich storehouse for the glory of the Creator and the relief of man's estate."

Francis Bacon

"Never mistake knowledge for wisdom. One helps you make a living; the other helps you make a life."

Sandra Carey

"That there should one man die ignorant who had capacity for knowledge, this I call a tragedy."

Thomas Carlyle

"Real knowledge is to know the extent of one's ignorance."

Confucius

"Knowledge is proud that he has learn'd so much; Wisdom is humble that he knows no more."

William Cowper

"In your thirst for knowledge, be sure not to drown in all the information."

Anthony D'Angelo

"Never stop learning; knowledge doubles every fourteen months."

Anthony D'Angelo

"Nurture your mind with great thoughts, for you will never go any higher than you think."

Benjamin Disraeli

"Knowledge is an antidote to fear."

Ralph Waldo Emerson

"Anyone who stops learning is old, whether twenty or eighty. Anyone who keeps learning today is young. The greatest thing in life is to keep your mind young."

Henry Ford

"Knowledge of our duties is the most essential part of the philosophy of life. If you escape duty you avoid action. The world demands results."

George W. Goethals

"Head knowledge is good, but heart knowledge is indispensable. The training of the hands and feet must be added to make a rounded education. We must all learn these days to become spiritual pioneers if we would save the world from chaos."

E. V. Hammond

"When a person is groping in life, we say "he has not found himself." This statement is not accurate. Self is created, not found."

Grant von Harrison

"It is the province of knowledge to speak and it is the privilege of wisdom to listen."

Oliver Wendell Holmes

"The great end of life is not knowledge but action."
T.H. Huxley

"If you want to be truly successful invest in yourself to get the knowledge you need to find your unique factor. When you find it and focus on it and persevere your success will blossom."
Sidney Madweb

"As knowledge increases, wonder deepens."
Charles Morgan

"Read every day something no one else is reading. Think every day something no one else is thinking. It is bad for the mind to be always part of unanimity."
Christopher Darlington Morley

"No matter where we begin, if we pursue knowledge diligently and honestly our quest will inevitably lead us from the things of earth to the things of heaven."
Hugh Nibley

"True knowledge never shuts the door on more knowledge, but zeal often does."
Hugh Nibley

"Knowledge does not come to us in details, but in flashes of light from heaven."
Henry David Thoreau

"Knowledge is the frontier of tomorrow."

Denis Waitley

"I not only use all the brains I have but all that I can borrow."

Woodrow Wilson

"Whatever is expressed is impressed. Whatever you say to yourself, with emotion, generates thoughts, ideas and behaviors consistent with those words."

Brian Tracy

"In times of change the learners shall inherit the earth, while the learned find themselves beautifully equipped to deal with a world that no longer exists."

Eric Hoffer

Leadership

"Leadership is influence."

John C. Maxwell

"A good objective of leadership is to help those who are doing poorly to do well and to help those who are doing well to do even better."

Jim Rohn

"Contrary to the old saying that leaders are born not made, the art of leading can be taught and it can be mastered."

General Mark W. Clark

"The boss drives people; the leader coaches them. The boss depends on authority; the leader on good will. The boss inspires fear; the leader inspires enthusiasm. The boss says "I"; The leader says "WE". The boss fixes the blame for the breakdown; the leader fixes the breakdown. The boss says, "GO"; the leader says "LET'S GO!"

H. Gordon Selfridge

"Respect the man, and he will do the more."

James Howell

"Leaders aren't born, they are made. And they are made just like anything else, through hard work. And that's the price we'll have to pay to achieve that goal, or any goal."
Vince Lombardi

"I am personally convinced that one person can be a change catalyst, a "transformer" in any situation, any organization. Such an individual is yeast that can leaven an entire loaf. It requires vision, initiative, patience, respect, persistence, courage, and faith to be a transforming leader."
Stephen Covey

"A boss creates fear, a leader confidence. A boss fixes blame, a leader corrects mistakes. A boss knows all, a leader asks questions. A boss makes work drudgery, a leader makes it interesting. A boss is interested in himself or herself, a leader is interested in the group."
Russell H. Ewing

"One of the true tests of leadership is the ability to recognize a problem before it becomes an emergency."
Arnold Glasow

"People ask the difference between a leader and a boss. The leader works in the open, and the boss in covert. The leader leads, and the boss drives."
Theodore Roosevelt

"A good manager is a man who isn't worried about his own career but rather the careers of those who work for him."

Henry S. M. Burns

"The greatest administrators do not achieve production through constraints and limitations. They provide opportunities."

Lao-Tze

"A leader is best when people barely know he exists, when his work is done, his aim fulfilled, they will say: We did it ourselves."

Lao-Tze

"Never tell people how to do things. Tell them what to do and they will surprise you with their ingenuity."

George S. Patton

"A leader takes people where they want to go. A great leader takes people where they don't necessarily want to go, but ought to be."

Rosalynn Carter

"Do not follow where the path may lead. Go instead where there is no path and leave a trail."

Muriel Strode

"Leadership is getting someone to do what they don't want to do, to achieve what they want to achieve."

Tom Landry

"The challenge of leadership is to be strong, but not rude; be kind, but not weak; be bold, but not bully; be thoughtful, but not lazy; be humble, but not timid; be proud, but not arrogant; have humor, but without folly."

Jim Rohn

"The best executive is the one who has sense enough to pick good men to do what he wants done, and self-restraint enough to keep from meddling with them while they do it."

Theodore Roosevelt

"Outstanding leaders go out of their way to boost the self-esteem of their personnel. If people believe in themselves, it's amazing what they can accomplish."

Sam Walton

"You manage things; you lead people."

Rear Admiral Grace Murray Hopper

"No man will make a great leader who wants to do it all himself, or to get all the credit for doing it."

Andrew Carnegie

"Entrepreneurs are the forgotten heroes of America."

Ronald Reagan

"I have three precious things which I hold fast and prize. The first is gentleness; the second is frugality; the third is humility, which keeps me from putting myself before others. Be gentle and you can be bold; be frugal and you can be liberal; avoid putting yourself before others and you can become a leader among men."

Lao-Tze

"He who has never learned to obey cannot be a good commander."

Aristotle

"The key to successful leadership today is influence, not authority."

Ken Blanchard

"The first responsibility of a leader is to define reality. The last is to say thank you. In between, the leader is a servant."

Max DuPree

"Leadership is not magnetic personality - that can just as well be a glib tongue. It is not "making friends and influencing people" -- that is flattery. Leadership is lifting a person's vision to high sights, the raising of a person's performance to a higher standard, the building of a personality beyond its normal limitations."

Peter Drucker

"You do not lead by hitting people over the head - that's assault, not leadership."

Dwight Eisenhower

"Big jobs usually go to the men who prove their ability to outgrow small ones."

Ralph Waldo Emerson

"Trust men and they will be true to you; treat them greatly, and they will show themselves great."

Ralph Waldo Emerson

"The leader has to be practical and a realist, yet must talk the language of the visionary and the idealist."

Eric Hoffer

"Respect a man, he will do the more."

James Howell

"Lift, Lead and Love."

Spencer W. Kimball

"Rule a kingdom as though you were cooking a small fish -don't overdo it."

Lao-Tze

"To command is to serve, nothing more and nothing less."

Andre Malraux

"Leadership is an action, not a position."

Donald H. McGannon

"A leader is a dealer in hope."

Napoleon I

"Confidence is contagious. So is lack of confidence."

Michael O'Brien

"One measure of leadership is the caliber of people who choose to follow you."

Dennis A. Peer

"Leadership is the ability of a single individual through his or her actions to motivate others to higher levels of achievement."

F. G. "Buck" Rodgers

"Leadership is the challenge to be something more than average."

Jim Rohn

"Leadership is a potent combination of strategy and character. But if you must be without one, be without the strategy."

General H. Norman Schwarzkopf

"Men make history, and not the other way around. In periods where there is no leadership, society stands still. Progress occurs when courageous, skillful leaders seize the opportunity to change things for the better."

Harry S. Truman

"Winners get to the top and turn around to see those they have defeated. Leaders get to the top and turn around to help others achieve the same."

Dan Churches

"Nearly all men can stand adversity, but if you want to test a man's character give him power."

Abraham Lincoln

Love

"Someone has written, "Love is a verb." It requires doing -not just saying and thinking. The test is in what one does, how one acts, for love is conveyed in word and deed."

David B. Haight

"Life in abundance comes only through great love."

Elbert Hubbard

"Love is the immortal flow of energy that nourishes, extends and preserves. Its eternal goal is life."

Smiley Blanton

"Give love and unconditional acceptance to those you encounter, and notice what happens."

Dr. Wayne W. Dyer

"Duty makes us do things well, but love makes us do them beautifully."

Zig Ziglar

"Life without love is like a tree without blossom and fruit."

Kahlil Gibran

"Love of country is like love of woman - he loves her best who seeks to bestow on her the highest good."

Felix Adler

"Love is a great beautifier."

Louisa May Alcott

"Love should be a vehicle allowed to travel without limitations."

Marvin J. Ashton

"If a thing loves, it is infinite."

William Blake

"Take away love and our earth is a tomb."

Robert Browning

"Love . . . [is] a lack of personal selfishness."

Theodore M. Burton

"Death is a challenge. It tells us not to waste time . . . It tells us to tell each other right now that we love each other."

Leo F. Buscaglia

"The person who has earned love the least needs it the most."

F. Enzio Busche

"Love is a force more formidable than any other. It is invisible - it cannot be seen or measured, yet it is powerful enough to transform you in a moment, and offer you more joy than any material possession could."

Barbara DeAngelis

"We are all born for love. . . . It is the principle of existence, and its only end."

Benjamin Disraeli

"Sincere love is something that sacrifices-not something that indulges itself. Sincere love is responsible. It would never knowingly hurt, but would heal."

Richard L. Evans

"Immature love says, "I love you because I need you." Mature love says, "I need you because I love you."

Erich Fromm

"Love is the only sane and satisfactory answer to the problem of human existence.

Erich Fromm

"Love is the strongest force the world possesses, and yet it is the humblest imaginable."

Mahatma Gandhi

"Whenever you have truth it must be given with love, or the message and the messenger will be rejected."

Mahatma Gandhi

"Love is the greatest gift that one generation can leave to another."

Richard Garnett

"We must love one another. Only [by doing] so can our long years of toil and struggle reach full reward and we be crowned with life everlasting."

Susa Young Gates

"Love is the only flower that grows and blossoms without the aid of seasons."

Kahlil Gibran

"Love you know, seeks to make happy rather than to be happy."

Charles William Gordon

"Love is perhaps the only glimpse we are permitted of eternity."

Helen Hayes

"Love is the master key that opens the gates of happiness."

Oliver Wendell Holmes

"At the center of non-violence stands the principle of love."

Martin Luther King, Jr.

"The greatest happiness of life it the conviction that we are loved - loved for ourselves, or rather, loved in spite of ourselves."

Victor Hugo

"I believe that unarmed truth and unconditional love will have the final word in reality. That is why right, temporarily defeated, is stronger than evil triumphant."

Martin Luther King, Jr.

Opportunity

"A pessimist sees the difficulty in every opportunity; an optimist sees the opportunity in every difficulty."
Winston Churchill

"...good luck waits to come to that man who accepts opportunity."
George Clason

"Each problem has hidden in an opportunity so powerful that it literally dwarfs the problem. The greatest success stories were created by people who recognized a problem a turned it into an opportunity."
Joseph Sugarman

"In the middle of difficulty lies opportunity."
Albert Einstein

"A wise man will make more opportunities than he finds."
Francis Bacon

"Opportunity...often it comes in the form of misfortune, or temporary defeat."
Napoleon Hill

"Opportunities? They are all around us...there is power lying latent everywhere waiting for the observant eye to discover it."

Orison Swett Marden

"Nothing is more expensive than a missed opportunity."

H. Jackson Brown Jr.

"Opportunity dances with those who are ready on the dance floor."

H. Jackson Brown Jr.

"Too many people are thinking of security instead of opportunity. They seem more afraid of life than death."

James F. Byrnes

"Opportunity does not knock, it presents itself when you beat down the door."

Kyle Chandler

"The office of government is not to confer happiness, but to give men the opportunity to work out happiness for themselves."

William Channing

"Everyone has a fair turn to be as great as he pleases."

Jeremy Collier

"An empowered organization is one in which individuals have the knowledge, skill, desire, and opportunity to personally succeed in a way that leads to collective organizational success."

Stephen Covey

"The right man is the one who seizes the moment."

Johann Von Goethe

"Your big opportunity may be right where you are now."

Napoleon Hill

"It still holds true that man is most uniquely human when he turns obstacles into opportunities."

Eric Hoffer

"He who refuses to embrace a unique opportunity loses the prize as surely as if he had failed."

William James

"To improve the golden moment of opportunity and catch the good that is within our reach is the great art of life."

Samuel Johnson

"Life is often compared to a marathon, but I think it is more like being a sprinter; long stretches of hard work punctuated by brief moments in which we are given the opportunity to perform at our best."

Michael Johnson

"Trouble is only opportunity in work clothes."
Henry J. Kaiser

"When written in Chinese, the word 'crisis' is composed of two characters. One represents danger and the other represents opportunity."
John F. Kennedy

"Democracy is based upon the conviction that there are extraordinary possibilities in ordinary people."
Harry Emerson Fosdick

"There will always be a Frontier where there is an open mind and a willing hand."
Charles Kettering

"Entrepreneurs are simply those who understand that there is little difference between obstacle and opportunity and are able to turn both to their advantage."
Victor Kiam

"I believe that you tend to create your own blessings. You have to prepare yourself so that when opportunity comes, you're ready."
Oprah Winfrey

"Decision and determination are the engineer and fireman of our train to opportunity and success."
Burt Lawlor

"As the opportunity grows for unlimited growth and progress, the chances of failure increase. There is no such thing as a program that will provide security and growth and progress with no risk . . . even within the church. As freedom for unrestricted development is enhanced, the possibilities for failure are also increased. The risk factor is great."

Dean L. Larsen

"If a window of opportunity appears, don't pull down the shade."

Tom Peters

"It is often hard to distinguish between the hard knocks in life and those of opportunity."

Frederick Philipse

"Luck is what happens when preparation meets opportunity."

Lucius Annæus Seneca

"The more you seek security, the less of it you have. But the more you seek opportunity, the more likely it is that you will achieve the security that you desire."

Brian Tracy

"You and I can never do a kindness too soon, for we never know how soon it will be too late."

Ralph Waldo Emerson

"The meeting of preparation with opportunity generates the offspring we call luck."

Anthony Robbins

Performance

"Being relaxed, at peace with yourself, confident, emotionally neutral, loose, and free-floating - these are the keys to successful performance in almost everything."
Dr. Wayne W. Dyer

"There is nothing in all the world so satisfying as a task well done. There is no reward so pleasing as that which comes with the mastery of a difficult problem."
Gordon B. Hinckley

"The best antidote I know for worry is work. The best medicine for despair is service. The best cure for weariness is the challenge of helping someone who is even more tired."
Gordon B. Hinckley

"The major work of the world is not done by geniuses. It is done by ordinary people, with balance in their lives, who have learned to work in an extraordinary manner."
Gordon B. Hinckley

"One of the greatest values…is the virtue of honest work. Knowledge without labor is profitless. Knowledge with labor is genius."
Gordon B. Hinckley

"Work is the miracle by which talent is brought to the surface and dreams become reality."

Gordon B. Hinckley

"Slumps are like a soft bed. They're easy to get into and hard to get out of."

Johnny Bench

"You have to perform at a consistently higher level than others. That's the mark of a true professional."

Joe Paterno

"Apply yourself. Get all the education you can, but then, by God, do something. Don't just stand there, make something happen."

Lee Iacocca

"My motto was always to keep swinging. Whether I was in a slump or feeling badly or having trouble off the field, the only thing to do was keep swinging."

Hank Aaron

"The important thing is to dare to dream big, and then take action to make it come true."

Joe Girard

"An acre of performance is worth a whole world of promise."

William Dean Howells

"Don't waste life in doubts and fears; spend yourself on the work before you, well assured that the right performance of this hour's duties will be the best preparation for the hours or ages that follow it."

Ralph Waldo Emerson

"Diligence is the mother of good luck."

Benjamin Franklin

"The most practical, beautiful, workable philosophy in the world won't work—if you won't."

Zig Ziglar

"When we do more than we are paid to do, eventually we will be paid more for what we do."

Zig Ziglar

"It is our individual performances, no matter how humble our place in life may be, that will in the long run determine how well ordered the world may become."

Paul C. Packer

"Be fanatics. When it comes to being and doing and dreaming the best, be maniacs."

A.M. Rosenthal

"The man who does not take pride in his own performance performs nothing in which to take pride."

Thomas J. Watson

"You are not here merely to make a living. You are here in order to enable the world to live more amply, with greater vision, with a finer spirit of hope and achievement. You are here to enrich the world, and you impoverish yourself if you forget the errand."

Woodrow Wilson

"You don't concentrate on risks. You concentrate on results. No risk is too great to prevent the necessary job from getting done."

Charles Yeager

"What we think or what we believe is, in the end, of little consequence. The only thing of consequence is what we do."

John Ruskin

"No man, who continues to add something to the material, intellectual and moral well-being of the place in which he lives, is left long without proper reward."

Booker T. Washington

"The harder you work, the luckier you get."

Gary Player

"You can't build a reputation on what you're going to do."

Henry Ford

"The talent of success is nothing more than doing what you can do well, and doing well whatever you do…"

Henry W. Longfellow

Perseverance

"People of mediocre ability sometimes achieve outstanding success because they don't know when to quit. Most men succeed because they are determined to."
George Allen

"In the confrontation between the stream and the rock, the stream always wins- not through strength but by perseverance."
H. Jackson Brown, Jr.

"Through persistence and hard work, we can each unlock the potential God has given us. We have within us not only the capacity to accomplish great things but also the ability to do ordinary things in extraordinary ways."
Lloyd Newell

"Perseverance is more prevailing than violence; and many things which cannot be overcome when they are together, yield themselves up when taken little by little."
Plutarch

"Perseverance is not a long race; it is many short races one after another."
Walter Elliott

"When you get into a tight place and everything goes against you, till it seems as though you could not hang on a minute longer, never give up then, for that is just the place and time that the tide will turn."

Harriet Beecher Stowe

"Other people and things can stop you temporarily. You're the only one who can do it permanently."

Zig Ziglar

"It's not so important who starts the game but who finishes it."

John Wooden

"Most of the important things in the world have been accomplished by people who have kept on trying when there seemed to be no help at all."

Dale Carnegie

"All great masters are chiefly distinguished by the power of adding a second, a third, and perhaps a fourth step in a continuous line. Many a man has taken the first step. With every additional step you enhance immensely the value of your first."

Ralph Waldo Emerson

"Consider the postage stamp; its usefulness consists in the ability to stick to one thing until it gets there."

Josh Billings

"Some men give up their designs when they have almost reached the goal; while others, on the contrary, obtain a victory by exerting, at the last moment, more vigorous efforts than ever before."

Herodotus

"Nothing in the world can take the place of persistence. Talent will not; nothing is more common than unsuccessful men with talent. Genius will not; unrewarded genius is almost a proverb. Education will not; the world is full of educated derelicts. Persistence and determination alone are omnipotent. The slogan, 'press on' has solved, and always will solve, the problems of the human race."

Calvin Coolidge

"Success is not final, failure is not fatal: it is the courage to continue that counts."

Winston Churchill

"Success seems to be connected with action. Successful men keep moving. They make mistakes, but they don't quit."

Conrad Hilton

"If I had to select one quality, one personal characteristic that I regard as being most highly correlated with success, whatever the field, I would pick the trait of persistence. Determination. The will to endure to the end, to get knocked down seventy times and get up off the floor saying. "Here comes number seventy-one!"

Richard M. Devos

"Good ideas are not adopted automatically. They must be driven into practice with courageous patience."

Hyman Rickover

"For a righteous man falls seven times, and rises again."

[Proverbs 24:16] Bible

"He who asks of life nothing but the improvement of his own nature... is less liable than anyone else to miss and waste life."

Henri Frederic Amiel

"The horizon is out there somewhere, and you just keep chasing it, looking for it, and working for it."

Bob Dole

"Success seems to be largely a matter of hanging on after others have let go."

William Feather

". . . be thou faithful unto death, and I will give thee a crown of life."

[Revelations 2:10] Bible

". . . The race is not [always] to the swift, nor the battle to the strong. . ."

[Ecclesiastes 9:11] Bible

"One of the commonest mistakes and one of the costliest is thinking that success is due to some genius, some magic - something or other which we do not possess. Success is generally due to holding on, and failure to letting go. You decide to learn a language, study music, take a course of reading, train yourself physically. Will it be success or failure? It depends upon how much pluck and perseverance that word "decide" contains. The decision that nothing can overrule, the grip that nothing can detach will bring success.
Remember the Chinese proverb, "With time and patience, the mulberry leaf becomes satin."

Maltbie Davenport Babcock

"Pay as little attention to discouragement as possible. Plough ahead as a steamer does, rough or smooth - rain or shine. To carry your cargo and make your port is the point. "

Maltbie Davenport Babcock

"A man of sense is never discouraged by difficulties; he redoubles his industry and his diligence, he perseveres, and infallibly prevails at last."

Lord Chesterfield

"Don't be afraid of opposition. Remember, a kite rises against not with, the wind."

Hamilton Mabie

"Men fail much oftener from want of perseverance than from want of talent."

William Cobbett

"Even the woodpecker owes his success to the fact that he uses his head and keeps pecking away until he finishes the job he starts."

Coleman Cox

"So long as there is breath in me, that long will I persist. For now I know one of the greatest principles of success; if I persist long enough I will win."

Og Mandino

"Great is the art of beginning, but greater is the art of ending."

Henry W. Longfellow

"Never give up. Never, never give up!. We shall go on to the end."

Winston Churchill

"Sure I am of this, that you have only to endure to conquer. You have only to persevere to save yourselves."

Winston Churchill

"What counts is not necessarily the size of the dog in the fight - it's the size of the fight in the dog."

Dwight Eisenhower

"Perseverance is not a long race; it is many short races one after another."

Walter Elliott

"Good luck is another name for tenacity of purpose."
Ralph Waldo Emerson

"Don't let life discourage you; everyone who got where he is had to begin where he was."
Richard L. Evans

"No man is ever whipped, until he quits -- in his own mind."
Napoleon Hill

"Before success comes in any man's life he is sure to meet with much temporary defeat and, perhaps, some failures. When defeat overtakes a man, the easiest and most logical thing to do is to quit. That is exactly what the majority of men do."
Napoleon Hill

"Persistence is to the character of man as carbon is to steel."
Napoleon Hill

"The majority of men meet with failure because of their lack of persistence in creating new plans to take the place of those which fail."
Napoleon Hill

"Victory is always possible for the person who refuses to stop fighting."
Napoleon Hill

"What we do not see, what most of us never suspect of existing, is the silent but irresistible power which comes to the rescue of those who fight on in the face of discouragement."

Napoleon Hill

"There is no failure except in no longer trying."

Elbert Hubbard

"Great works are performed, not by strength, but by perseverance."

Samuel Johnson

"When Babe Didrickson Zaharias, often called the 'athletic phenomenon of all time,' won the British woman's gold tournament, people said of her what they had said many times before: "Oh, she's an automatic champion, a natural athlete." When Babe started golfing in earnest thirteen years ago she hit as many as 1,000 balls in one afternoon, playing until her hands were so sore they had to be taped."

James Keller

"Having chosen our course, without guile and with pure purpose, let us renew our trust in God, and go forward without fear and with manly hearts."

Abraham Lincoln

"Some people plant in the spring and leave in the summer. If you're signed up for a season, see it through. You don't have to stay forever, but at least stay until you see it through."

Jim Rohn

"Perseverance is a positive, active characteristic. It is not idly, passively waiting and hoping for some good thing to happen. It gives us hope by helping us realize that the righteous suffer no failure except in giving up and no longer trying. We must never give up, regardless of temptations, frustrations, disappointments, or discouragements."

Joseph B. Wirthlin

"You don't become enormously successful without encountering and overcoming a number of extremely challenging problems."

Mark Victor Hansen

"I learned about the strength you can get from a close family life. I learned to keep going, even in bad times. I learned not to despair, even when my world was falling apart. I learned that there are no free lunches. And I learned the value of hard work."

Lee Iacocca

"Defeat is simply a signal to press onward."

Helen Keller

"He that can heroically endure adversity will bear prosperity with equal greatness of soul; for the mind that cannot be dejected by the former is not likely to be transported with the latter."

Henry Fielding

"A leader, once convinced that a particular course of action is the right one, must....be undaunted when the going gets tough."

Ronald Reagan

"Patience and perseverance have a magical effect before which difficulties disappear and obstacles vanish."

John Quincy Adams

"Fight one more round. When your arms are so tired that you can hardly lift your hands to come on guard, fight one more round. When your nose is bleeding and your eyes are black and you are so tired that you wish your opponent would crack you one on the jaw and put you to sleep, fight one more round - remembering that the man who always fights one more round is never whipped."

James Corbett

"I do not think there is any other quality so essential to success of any kind as the quality of perseverance. It overcomes almost everything, even nature."

John D. Rockefeller

"Three great essentials to achieve anything worthwhile
are, first, hard work; second, stick-to-itiveness; third,
common sense."

Thomas Edison

Purpose

"We make a living by what we get, but we make a life by what we give."

Winston Churchill

"There is one quality that one must possess to win, and that is definiteness of purpose, the knowledge of what one wants, and a burning desire to possess it."

Napoleon Hill

"Nourish the mind like you would your body. The mind cannot survive on junk food."

Jim Rohn

"We all have two choices: We can make a living or we can design a life."

Jim Rohn

"One person caring about another represents life's greatest value."

Jim Rohn

"Giving is better than receiving because giving starts the receiving process."

Jim Rohn

"Sharing makes you bigger than you are. The more you pour out, the more life will be able to pour in."

Jim Rohn

"You can have everything in life you want, if you will just help enough other people get what they want."

Zig Ziglar

"Set peace of mind as your highest goal and organize your entire life around it."

Brian Tracy

"You cannot make it as a wandering generality. You must become a meaningful specific."

Zig Ziglar

"The kindest thing you can do for the people you care about is to become a happy, joyous person."

Brian Tracy

"Happiness and high performance come to you when you choose to live your life consistent with your highest values and your deepest convictions."

Brian Tracy

"Happiness comes when you believe in what you are doing, know what you are doing, and live what you are doing."

Brian Tracy

"Don't be reluctant to give of yourself generously, it's the mark of caring and compassion and personal greatness."

Brian Tracy

"We are at our very best, and we are happiest, when we are fully engaged in work we enjoy on the journey toward the goal we've established for ourselves. It gives meaning to our time off and comfort to our sleep. It makes everything else in life so wonderful, so worthwhile."

Earl Nightingale

"Those valleys of discouragement make more beautiful the peaks of achievement."

Gordon B. Hinckley

"Generally speaking, the most miserable people I know are those who are obsessed with themselves; the happiest people I know are those who lose themselves in the service of others...

"By and large, I have come to see that if we complain about life, it is because we are thinking only of ourselves."

Gordon B. Hinckley

"What a therapeutic and wonderful thing it is for a man or woman to set aside all consideration of personal gain and reach out with strength and energy and purpose to help the unfortunate, to improve the community, to clean up the environment, and to beautify our surroundings."

Gordon B. Hinckley

"He who waits to do a great deal of good at once, will never do anything."

Samuel Johnson

"Always be loyal to those who are absent, if you want to retain those who are present."

Stephen Covey

"We who lived in concentration camps can remember those who walked through the huts comforting others, giving away their last piece of bread. They may have been few in number, but they offer sufficient proof that everything can be taken from a person but the last of the human freedoms - to choose one's attitude in any given set of circumstances - to choose one's own way."

Viktor Frankl

"A man who becomes conscious of the responsibility he bears toward a human being who affectionately waits for him, or to an unfinished work, will never be able to throw away his life. He knows the why for his existence, and will be able to bear almost any how."

Viktor Frankl

"A person who won't stand for something will fall for anything."

Zig Ziglar

"Show me someone who has done something worthwhile, and I'll show you someone who has overcome adversity."

Lou Holtz

"To be accounted trustworthy, a person must be predictable. When you manage your life and all the little decisions by one guideline--the Golden Rule--you create an ethical predictability in your life. People will have confidence in you, knowing that you consistently do the right thing."

John C. Maxwell

"I have one life and one chance to make it count for something... I'm free to choose what that something is, and the something I've chosen is my faith. Now, my faith goes beyond theology and religion and requires considerable work and effort. My faith demands -- this is not optional – my faith demands that I do whatever I can, wherever I am, whenever I can, for as long as I can with whatever I have to try to make a difference."

Jimmy Carter

"I can't believe that God put us on this earth to be ordinary."

Lou Holtz

"Happiness is not the result of circumstance. It is the result of loving others."

Lloyd Newell

"I expect to pass through life but once. If, therefore, there be any kindness I can show, or any good thing I can do to any fellow being, let me do it now, for I shall not pass this way again."

William Penn

"To better the lives of others is one of your life's greatest rewards."

Captain Len Kaine US Navy (retired)
President Golden Rule Society

"In a gentle way, you can shake the world."

Mahatma Gandhi

"If I cannot do great things, I can do small things in a great way."

James F. Clarke

"No man is worth his salt who is not ready at al times to risk his well-being, to risk his body, to risk his life, in a great cause."

Theodore Roosevelt

"Caring comes from being able to put yourself in the position of the other person. If you cannot imagine, 'This might happen to me,' you are able to say to yourself with indifference, 'Who cares?'"

Eleanor Roosevelt

"What basic objective I had, for many years, was to grasp every opportunity to live and experience life as deeply, as fully, and as widely as I possibly could."

Eleanor Roosevelt

"We begin from the recognition that all beings cherish happiness and do not want suffering. It then becomes both morally wrong and pragmatically unwise to pursue only one's own happiness oblivious to the feelings and aspirations of all others who surround us as members of the same human family. The wiser course is to think of others when pursuing our own happiness."

Dalai Lama

"Life is not worth living unless it is lived for others."

Mother Teresa

"The biggest disease today is not leprosy or cancer or tuberculosis, but rather the feeling of being unwanted, uncared for, deserted by everybody. The greatest evil is the lack of love and charity, the terrible indifference towards one's neighbor."

Mother Teresa

"The impersonal hand of government can never replace the helping hand of a neighbor."

Hubert Humphrey

"Lack of something to feel important about is almost the greatest tragedy a man may have."

Arthur E. Morgan

"We pay a price when we deprive children of the exposure to the values, principles, and education they need to make them good citizens."

Sandra Day O'Connor

"Happiness...that's something you can't achieve by taking the easy way out. Earning happiness means doing good and working, not speculating and being lazy. Laziness may look inviting, but only work gives you true satisfaction."

Anne Frank

"I shall not remain insignificant, I shall work in the world for mankind....I don't want to have lived in vain like most people. I want to be useful or bring enjoyment to all people, even those I've never met. I want to go on living, even after my death!"

Anne Frank

"Anybody who believes in something without reservation believes that this thing is right and should be, has the stamina to meet obstacles and overcome them."

Golda Meir

"I see so many of my kind who have gone mad for want of something to do."

Florence Nightingale

"I only wish I could work to some purpose....I have no right to these easy comfortable days and our poor men suffering and dying thirsting in this hot sun and I so quiet here in want of nothing."

Clara Barton

"If you would find happiness and joy, lose your life in some noble cause. A worthy purpose must be at the center of every worthy life."

Jack H. Goaslind, Jr.

"Success has nothing to do with what you gain in life or accomplish for yourself. It's what you do for others."

Danny Thomas

"Many persons have a wrong idea of what constitutes true happiness. It is not attained through self-gratification but through fidelity to a worthy purpose."

Helen Keller

"It is one of the beautiful compensations of this life that no one can sincerely try to help another without helping himself."

Charles Dudley Warner

"Happiness is like a kiss. You must share it to enjoy it."

Bernard Melzer

"Generous people are rarely mentally ill people"

Karl Menninger

"The service we render others is really the rent we pay for our room on Earth.

Wilfred Grenfell

"No person was ever honored for what he received. Honor has been the reward for what he gave."

Calvin Coolidge

"Efforts and courage are not enough without purpose and direction."

John F. Kennedy

"Give a man health and a course to steer, and he'll never stop to trouble about whether he's happy or not.

George Bernard Shaw

"Man needs difficulties; they are necessary for health."

Carl Jung

"One thing I know: the only ones among you who will be really happy are those who will have sought and found how to serve."

Albert Schweitzer

"Far better it is to dare mighty things, to win glorious triumphs, even though checkered by failure, than to take rank with those poor spirits who neither enjoy much nor suffer much, because they live in the grey twilight that knows not victory nor defeat."

Theodore Roosevelt

"Lose no time; be always employed in something useful."

Benjamin Franklin

"In the time we have it is surely our duty to do all the good we can to all the people we can in all the ways we can."

William Barclay

"We must give more in order to get more. It is the generous giving of ourselves that produce the generous harvest."

Orison Swett Marden

Success

"The great successful men of the world have used their imagination...they think ahead and create their mental picture in all its details, filling in here, adding a little there, altering this a bit and that a bit, but steadily building - steadily building."

Robert Collier

"When a man feels throbbing within him the power to do what he undertakes as well as it can possibly be done, this is happiness, this is success."

Orison Swett Marden

"Success means accomplishments as the result of our own efforts and abilities. Proper preparation is the key to our success. Our acts can be no wiser than our thoughts. Our thinking can be no wiser than our understanding."

George Clason

"Success doesn't come to you...you go to it."

Marva Collins

"Success is simply a matter of luck. Ask any failure."

Earl Nightingale

"People become really quite remarkable when they start thinking that they can do things. When they believe in themselves they have the first secret of success."

Norman Vincent Peale

"Man was designed for accomplishment, engineered for success, and endowed with the seeds of greatness."

Zig Ziglar

"Success is not measured by what you do compared to what others do, it is measured by what you do with the ability God gave you."

Zig Ziglar

"The difference between a successful person and others is not a lack of strength, not a lack of knowledge, but rather in a lack of will."

Vincent Lombardi

"Success is a journey, not a destination."

Ben Sweetland

"The difference between failure and success is doing a thing nearly right and doing a thing exactly right."

Edward Simmons

"Our limitations and success will be based, most often, on your own expectations for ourselves. What the mind dwells upon, the body acts upon."

Denis Waitley

"Desire is the key to motivation, but it's the determination and commitment to an unrelenting pursuit of your goal – a commitment to excellence - that will enable you to attain the success you seek."

Mario Andretti

"No one ever attains very eminent success by simply doing what is required of him; it is the amount and excellence of what is over and above the required that determines the greatness of ultimate distinction."

Charles Kendall Adams

"The secret of success in life is for a man to be ready for his opportunity when it comes."

Benjamin Disraeli

"It takes time to succeed because success is merely the natural reward of taking time to do anything well."

Joseph Ross

"I believe the greater the handicap, the greater the triumph."

John H. Johnson

"My list of ingredients for success is divided into four basic groups: Inward, Outward, Upward and Onward."

David Thomas

"Possession of the ball is the key to winning in football, basketball, and the game of life."

Laing Burns, Jr.

"Success often comes to those who have the aptitude to see way down the road."

Laing Burns, Jr.

"Enthusiasm is the highest paid quality on earth."

Frank Bettger

"There's no limit to what a man can achieve, if he doesn't care who gets the credit."

Laing Burns, Jr.

"Unless you're willing to have a go, fail miserably, and have another go, success won't happen."

Phillip Adams

"Health, happiness and success depend upon the fighting spirit of each person. The big thing is not what happens to us in life - but what we do about what happens to us."

George Allen

"The worst bankrupt in the world is the man who has lost his enthusiasm. Let a man lose everything else in the world but his enthusiasm and he will come through again to success."

H.W. Arnold

"One important key to success is self-confidence. An important key to self-confidence is preparation."

Arthur Ashe

"Keep in mind that neither success nor failure is ever final."

Roger Ward Babson

· "I was made to work. If you are equally industrious, you will be equally successful."

Johann Sebastian Bach

"If there is any one axiom that I have tried to live up to in trying to become successful in business, it is the fact that I have tried to surround myself with associates that know more about business than I do. This policy has always been very successful and is still working for me."

Monte L. Bean

"Shallow men believe in luck. Strong men believe in cause and effect."

Ralph Waldo Emerson

"The toughest thing about success is that you've got to keep on being a success. Talent is only a starting point in business. You've got to keep working that talent."

Irving Berlin

"The victory of success is half won when one gains the habit of work."

Sarah Knowles Bolton

"Don't confuse fame with success. Madonna is one; Helen Keller is the other."

Erma Bombeck

"Successful men are influenced by desire for pleasing results. Failures are influenced by desire for pleasing methods."

Frank E. Brennan

"The people who get on in this world are the people who get up and look for the circumstances they want and, if they can't find them, make them."

George Bernard Shaw

"Success is a state of mind. If you want success, start thinking of yourself as a success."

Dr. Joyce Brothers

"Men are failures, not because they are stupid, but because they are not sufficiently impassioned."

Struther Burt

"Experience shows that success is due less to ability than to zeal. The winner is he who gives himself to his work, body and soul."

Sir Thomas Fowell Buxton

"The road to success is not to be run upon by seven leagued boots. Step by step, little by little, bit by bit-that is the way to wealth that is the way to wisdom that is the way to glory."

Sir Thomas Fowell Buxton

"Success in business implies optimism, mutual confidence, and fair play. A business man must hold a high opinion of the worth of what he has to sell and he must feel that he is a useful public servant."

R.H. Cabell

"Success is not the key to happiness. Happiness is the key to success. If you love what you are doing, you will be successful."

Herman Cain

"The important thing to recognize is that it takes a team, and the team ought to get credit for the wins and the losses. Successes have many fathers, failures have none."

Philip Caldwell

"Failure is the condiment that gives success its flavor."

Truman Capote

"I believe that the true road to preeminent success in any line is to make yourself master of that line."

Andrew Carnegie

"People rarely succeed unless they have fun in what they are doing."

Dale Carnegie

"Success is getting what you want; happiness is wanting what you get."

Dale Carnegie

"When you have much success, two things happen. The first is that we begin to take success for granted. The second is that we forget how we got here-namely, by exceptionally hard work and in spite of intense competition."

Jack Mack Carter

"Destiny is not a matter of chance, it is a matter of choice; it is not a thing to be waited for, it is a thing to be achieved."

Winston Churchill

"There is but one straight road to success, and that is merit. The man who is successful is the man who is useful. Capacity never lacks opportunity. It can not remain undiscovered, because it is sought by too many anxious to use it."

Bourke Cockran

"Success depends upon previous preparation, and without such preparation there is sure to be failure."

Confucius

"An empowered organization is one in which individuals have the knowledge, skill, desire, and opportunity to personally succeed in a way that leads to collective organizational success."

Stephen Covey

"To me success would be to be able to do your very best in everything you do."

Paul Cummings

"In order to succeed you must fail, so that you know what not to do the next time."

Anthony D'Angelo

"History records the successes of men with objectives and a sense of direction. Oblivion is the position of small men overwhelmed by obstacles."

William Danforth

"Somehow I can't believe there are many heights that can't be scaled by a man who knows the secret of making dreams come true. This special secret can be summarized in four C's. They are: curiosity, confidence, courage, and constancy, and the greatest of these is confidence."

Walt Disney

"Many of life's failures are people who did not realize how close they were to success when they gave up."

Thomas Edison

"If A equal success, then the formula is A equals X plus Y and Z, with X being work, Y play, and Z keeping your mouth shut."

Albert Einstein

"Try not to become a man of success, but rather to become a man of value. He is considered successful in our day who gets more out of life than he puts in. But a man of value will give more than he receives."

Albert Einstein

"Self-trust is the first secret of success."

Ralph Waldo Emerson

"Success has a simple formula: do your best, and people may like it."

Sam Ewing

"What is the recipe for successful achievement? To my mind there are just four essential ingredients: Choose a career you love . . . Give it the best there is in you . . . Seize your opportunities And be a member of the team. In no country but America, I believe, is it possible to fulfill all four of these requirements."

Benjamin Fairless

"The great dividing line between success and failure can be expressed in five words: "I did not have time."

Franklin Field

"Success as I see it, is a result, not a goal."

Gustave Flaubert

"History has demonstrated that the most notable winners usually encountered heart-breaking obstacles before they triumphed. They won because they refused to become discouraged by their defeats."

B.C. Forbes

"Failure is success if we learn from it."

Malcolm Forbes

"The man who will use his skill and constructive imagination to see how much he can give for a dollar, instead of how little he can give for a dollar, is bound to succeed."

Henry Ford

"Good is not good where better is expected."

Thomas Fuller

"A great pleasure in life is doing what people say you cannot do."

Walter Gagehot

"No one can possibly achieve any real and lasting success or "get rich" in business by being a conformist."

J. Paul Getty

"Success is always temporary. When all is said and done, the only thing you'll have left is your character."

Vince Gill

"Men give me credit for some genius. All the genius I have lies in this: When I have a subject in hand, I study it profoundly. Day and night it is before me. I explore it in all its bearings. My mind becomes pervaded with it. Then the effort which I have made is what people are pleased to call the fruit of genius. It is the fruit of labor and thought."

Alexander Hamilton

"Many a one has succeeded only because he has failed after repeated efforts. If he had never met defeat, he would never have known any great victory."

Orison Swett Marden

"You can do anything you wish to do, have anything you wish to have, be anything you wish to be."

Robert Collier

"Every minute you spend in planning saves 10 minutes in execution; this gives you a 1,000 percent return on energy!"

Brian Tracy

"The men who succeed best in public life are those who take the risk of standing by their own convictions."

James Garfield

"Achievement seems to be connected with action. Successful men and women keep moving. They make mistakes, but they don't quit."

Conrad Hilton

"You don't become enormously successful without encountering and overcoming a number of extremely challenging problems."

Mark Victor Hansen

"Personal development is your springboard to personal excellence. Ongoing, continuous, non-stop personal development literally assures you that there is no limit to what you can accomplish."

Brian Tracy

"History knows no resting places and no plateaus."

Henry Kissinger

"Time is our most valuable asset, yet we tend to waste it, kill it, and spend it rather than invest it."

Jim Rohn

"I can promise you that the challenges you'll meet on the road to success are far less difficult to deal with than the struggles and the disappointments that come from being average."

Jim Rohn

"The indispensable first step to getting the things you want out of life is this: decide what you want."

Ben Stein

"I do not think there is any other quality so essential to success of any kind as the quality of perseverance. It overcomes almost everything, even nature."

John D. Rockefeller

"The successful person has the habit of doing the things failures don't like to do. They don't like doing them either necessarily. But their disliking is subordinated to the strength of their purpose."

E.M. Gray

"Behold the turtle. He makes progress only when he sticks his neck out."

James B. Conant

"If you advance confidently in the direction of your dreams, and endeavor to live the life which you have imagined, you will meet with a success unexpected in common hours."

Henry David Thoreau

Teamwork

"Teamwork is the ability to work together toward a common vision. The ability to direct individual accomplishments toward organizational objectives. It is the fuel that allows common people to attain uncommon results."

Andrew Carnegie

"Alone we can do so little; together we can do so much."

Helen Keller

"Coming together is a beginning, staying together is progress, and working together is success."

Henry Ford

"The achievements of an organization are the results of the combined effort of each individual."

Vince Lombardi

"People have been known to achieve more as a result of working with others than against them."

Dr. Allan Fromme

"It is literally true that you can succeed best and quickest by helping others to succeed."

Napoleon Hill

"If a team is to reach its potential, each player must be willing to subordinate his personal goals to the good of the team."

Bud Wilkinson

"When your team is winning, be ready to be tough, because winning can make you soft. On the other hand, when you team is losing, stick by them. Keep believing."

Bo Schembechler

"The way a team plays as a whole determines its success. You may have the greatest bunch of individual stars in the world, but if they don't play together, the club won't be worth a dime."

Babe Ruth

"In order to become a leading home run hitter, a batter must be surrounded by good hitters, otherwise, the pitchers will 'pitch around' him. Likewise, many successful people became that way from being on a good team."

Laing Burns Jr.

"Teamwork is neither "good" nor "desirable." It is a fact. Wherever people work together or play together they do so as a team. Which team to use for what purpose is a crucial, difficult and risky decision that is even harder to unmake. Managements have yet to learn how to make it."

Peter Drucker

"Individual commitment to a group effort - that is what makes a team work, a company work, a society work, a civilization work."

Vince Lombardi

"Finding good players is easy. Getting them to play as a team is another story."

Casey Stengel

"Many of us are more capable than some of us . . . but none of us is as capable as all of us!!"

Tom Wilson

"Lots of people want to ride with you in the limo, but what you want is someone who will take the bus with you when the limo breaks down."

Oprah Winfrey

Victory

"There are important cases in which the difference between half a heart and a whole heart makes just the difference between signal defeat and a splendid victory."

A.H.K. Boyd

"The ultimate victory in competition is derived from the inner satisfaction of knowing that you have done your best and that you have gotten the most out of what you had to give."

Howard Cosell

"Men talk as if victory were something fortunate. Work is victory."

Ralph Waldo Emerson

"I would rather lose in a cause that will some day win, than win in a cause that will some day lose!"

Woodrow Wilson

"Accept the challenges, so that you may feel the exhilaration of victory."

General George Patton

"It is not enough to fight. It is the spirit which we bring to the fight that decides the issue. It is morale that wins the victory."

General George Marshall

"Far better it is to dare mighty things, to win glorious triumphs, even though checkered by failure, than to take rank with those poor spirits who neither enjoy much nor suffer much, because they live in the grey twilight that knows not victory nor defeat."

Theodore Roosevelt

Will Power

"The man who goes farthest is generally the one who is willing to do and dare. The sure-thing boat never gets far from shore."

Dale Carnegie

"You have a very powerful mind that can make anything happen as long as you keep yourself centered."

Dr. Wayne W. Dyer

"Strength does not come from physical capacity. It comes from an indomitable will."

Mahatma Gandhi

"People do not lack strength; they lack will."

Victor Hugo

"What you have to do and the way you have to do it is incredibly simple. Whether you are willing to do it, that's another matter."

Peter Drucker

"Will is character in action."

William Mcdougall

"They can conquer who believe they can. He has not learned the first lesson is life who does not every day surmount a fear."

Ralph Waldo Emerson

"The time is always right to do what is right."

Martin Luther King Jr.

"Your own mind is a sacred enclosure into which nothing harmful can enter except by your promotion."

Ralph Waldo Emerson

Appendix A – Links

Ordinary People Can Win!
http://www.ordinarypeoplecanwin.com/

Ordinary People Can Win free, weekly e-zine
http://www.ordinarypeoplecanwin.com/ezinepage.htm

Ordinary People Can Win free achievement e-course
ordinarypeople@getresponse.com

James Allen
http://www.ordinarypeoplecanwin.com/jamesallen.htm

Ezra Taft Benson
http://www.ordinarypeoplecanwin.com/ezrataftbenson.htm

Kenneth Blanchard
http://www.ordinarypeoplecanwin.com/kennethblanchard.htm

H. Jackson Brown, Jr.
http://www.ordinarypeoplecanwin.com/hjacksonbrownjr.htm

Hugh B. Brown
http://www.ordinarypeoplecanwin.com/hughbbrown.htm

Les Brown
http://www.ordinarypeoplecanwin.com/lesbrown.htm

Dale Carnegie
http://www.ordinarypeoplecanwin.com/dalecarnegie.htm

Jimmy Carter
http://www.ordinarypeoplecanwin.com/jimmycarter.htm

Winston Churchill
http://www.ordinarypeoplecanwin.com/winstonchurchill.htm

George Clason
http://www.ordinarypeoplecanwin.com/georgeclason.htm

Dr. Stephen R. Covey
http://www.ordinarypeoplecanwin.com/stephenrcovey.htm

Hugh Downs
http://www.ordinarypeoplecanwin.com/hughdowns.htm

Peter Drucker
http://www.ordinarypeoplecanwin.com/peterdrucker.htm

Henry Drummond
http://www.ordinarypeoplecanwin.com/henrydrummond.htm

Dr. Wayne Dyer
http://www.ordinarypeoplecanwin.com/waynedyer.htm

Henry B. Eyring
http://www.ordinarypeoplecanwin.com/henrybeyring.htm

Benjamin Fairless
http://www.ordinarypeoplecanwin.com/benjaminffairless.htm

Viktor Frankl
http://www.ordinarypeoplecanwin.com/viktorfrankl.htm

Mahatma Gandhi
http://www.ordinarypeoplecanwin.com/gandhi.htm

Heber J. Grant
http://www.ordinarypeoplecanwin.com/heberjgrant.htm

Mark Victor Hansen
http://www.ordinarypeoplecanwin.com/markvictorhansen.htm

Napoleon Hill
http://www.ordinarypeoplecanwin.com/napoleonhill.htm

Gordon B. Hinckley
http://www.ordinarypeoplecanwin.com/gordonbhinckley.htm

Lou Holtz
http://www.ordinarypeoplecanwin.com/louholtz.htm

Howard W. Hunter
http://www.ordinarypeoplecanwin.com/howardwhunter.htm

Jack Kinder
http://www.ordinarypeoplecanwin.com/jackkinder.htm

Dr. Martin Luther King, Jr.
http://www.ordinarypeoplecanwin.com/martinlutherkingjr.htm

C. S. Lewis
http://www.ordinarypeoplecanwin.com/cslewis.htm

Art Linkletter
http://www.ordinarypeoplecanwin.com/artlinkletter.htm

David O. MacKay
http://www.ordinarypeoplecanwin.com/davidomackay.htm

Harvey Mackay
http://www.ordinarypeoplecanwin.com/harveymackay.htm

Og Mandino
http://www.ordinarypeoplecanwin.com/ogmandino.htm

Orison Swett Marden
http://www.ordinarypeoplecanwin.com/orisonswettmarden.htm

John C. Maxwell
http://www.ordinarypeoplecanwin.com/johncmaxwell.htm

Foster C. McClellan
http://www.ordinarypeoplecanwin.com/fostercmcclellan.htm

Lloyd Newell
http://www.ordinarypeoplecanwin.com/lloydnewell.htm

Hugh Nibley
http://www.ordinarypeoplecanwin.com/hughnibley.htm

Earl Nightengale
http://www.ordinarypeoplecanwin.com/earlnightengale.htm

Norman Vincent Peale
http://www.ordinarypeoplecanwin.com/normanvincentpeale.htm

Tom Peters
http://www.ordinarypeoplecanwin.com/tompeters.htm

Anthony Robbins
http://www.ordinarypeoplecanwin.com/anthonyrobbins.htm

Eddie Robinson
http://www.ordinarypeoplecanwin.com/eddierobinson.htm

Jim Rohn
http://www.ordinarypeoplecanwin.com/jimrohn.htm

Robert Schuller
http://www.ordinarypeoplecanwin.com/roberschuller.htm

Hans Selye
http://www.ordinarypeoplecanwin.com/hansselye.htm

Charles Swindoll
http://www.ordinarypeoplecanwin.com/charlesswindoll.htm

Henry David Thoreau
http://www.ordinarypeoplecanwin.com/henrydavidthoreau.htm

Brian Tracy
http://www.ordinarypeoplecanwin.com/briantracy.htm

Mark Twain
http://www.ordinarypeoplecanwin.com/marktwain.htm

Denis Waitley
http://www.ordinarypeoplecanwin.com/deniswaitley.htm

Carolyn Warner
http://www.ordinarypeoplecanwin.com/carolynwarner.htm

John Wooden
http://www.ordinarypeoplecanwin.com/johnwooden.htm

Zig Ziglar
http://www.ordinarypeoplecanwin.com/zigziglar.htm

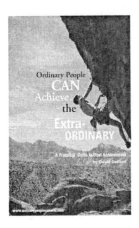

Ordinary People Can Achieve the Extraordinary—
A Practical Guide to Goal Achievement
by David DeFord

If you are ready to jump off of the New Year's resolution cycle and begin to really achieve your dreams, this is the book for you!

David DeFord has written the book you need to accomplish all that you seek in your life.

Ordinary People Can Achieve the Extraordinary-A Practical Guide to Goal Achievement will help you surpass the inevitable obstacles. In the past, you became discouraged and quit chasing your dreams.
Now, you can press past these roadblocks and reach your chosen destinations.

Learn:
- How to finally take control of your future
- How to build foundations under your dreams
- How you no longer need to "settle" for what you have
- Why living the "TV Existence" kills your dreams, and how to break free
- The best way to select your goals
- How to identify your "Great One Thing"
- How to use all of your sense to keep enthused
- How to become the success you seek
- How to deserve it

- Some simple record-keeping techniques to measure your progress
- How to talk yourself into overcoming the temptation to backslide
- How keeping a journal will help you succeed
- Resources that can help you keep your determination high
- Free e-zines to instruct and inspire you
- Discussion groups and forums that can help you
- How giving back to your community helps you deserve abundance

"*Ordinary People Can Achieve the Extraordinary*" is an inspiring book that enables the reader to realise that their dreams are achievable and can be accomplished. It is a fully descriptive process for help in achieving one's dreams. "Change your approach, not your dreams" is an awesome statement. I like the way you have used examples to express your meaning and also many other resources to follow."
Michelle Peterson, Professional Organizer (New Zealand)

Purchase it on Amazon.com or order it here:

I want _____ copies of Ordinary People Can Achieve the Extraordinary for $14.00 each.

I want _____ copies of 1000 Brilliant Achievement Quotes for $14.00 each.

Include $2.00 shipping and handling for one book, and $1.00 for each additional book. Nebraska residents much include $.98 sales tax per book.

My check or money order for $_____ is enclosed.
Please charge my __ Visa __ Mastercard __ American Express

Name _____

Address _____

City/State/Zip _____

Email _____

Card # _____ Exp Date _____

Signature _____

Mail payment to:

Ordinary People Can Win! 13964 Margo Street Omaha, NE 68138

http://www.OrdinaryPeopleCanWin.com